300 CALORIE

recipes

Eat great and lose weight with these satisfying recipes for any meal

pil

Publications International, Ltd.

Favorite Brand Name Recipes is a trademark of Publications International, Ltd.

Pictured on the front cover *(clockwise from top left):* Tuscan Turkey and White Bean Skillet *(page 66)*, Chunky Black Bean and Sweet Potato Chili *(page 92)*, Zesty Pasta Salad *(page 156)*, Artichoke, Olive and Goat Cheese Pizza *(page 82)* and Creamy Cappuccino Frozen Dessert *(page 162)*.

Pictured on the back cover *(left to right):* Oatmeal Banana Pancakes *(page 22)* and Berry Bundt Cake *(page 186)*.

ISBN-13: 978-1-4508-5441-2
ISBN-10: 1-4508-5441-9

Library of Congress Control Number: 2012935919

Manufactured in China.

8 7 6 5 4 3 2 1

Nutritional Analysis: Every effort has been made to check the accuracy of the nutritional information that appears with each recipe. However, because numerous variables account for a wide range of values for certain foods, nutritive analyses in this book should be considered approximate. Different results may be obtained by using different nutrient databases and different brand-name products.

Microwave Cooking: Microwave ovens vary in wattage. Use the cooking times as guidelines and check for doneness before adding more time.

Note: This publication is only intended to provide general information. The information is specifically not intended to be a substitute for medical diagnosis or treatment by your physician or other health care professional. You should always consult your own physician or other health care professionals about any medical questions, diagnosis, or treatment. (Products vary among manufacturers. Please check labels carefully to confirm nutritional values.)

The information obtained by you from this book should not be relied upon for any personal, nutritional, or medical decision. You should consult an appropriate professional for specific advice tailored to your specific situation. PIL makes no representations or warranties, express or implied, with respect to your use of this information.

In no event shall PIL, its affiliates or advertisers be liable for any direct, indirect, punitive, incidental, special, or consequential damages, or any damages whatsoever including, without limitation, damages for personal injury, death, damage to property, or loss of profits, arising out of or in any way connected with the use of any of the above-referenced information or otherwise arising out of the use of this book.

pil

Publications International, Ltd.

Contents

Breakfast

oatmeal with maple-glazed apples and cranberries

3 cups water

¼ teaspoon salt

2 cups quick or old-fashioned oats

1 teaspoon unsalted butter

¼ teaspoon ground cinnamon

2 medium red or golden delicious apples, unpeeled, cut into ½-inch chunks

2 tablespoons sugar-free maple syrup

4 tablespoons dried cranberries

1. Bring water and salt to a boil in large saucepan. Stir in oats; reduce heat and simmer 1 to 2 minutes for quick oats or 5 to 6 minutes for old-fashioned oats.

2. Meanwhile, melt butter in large nonstick skillet over medium heat; stir in cinnamon. Add apples; cook and stir 4 to 5 minutes or until tender. Stir in maple syrup until heated through.

3. Spoon oatmeal evenly into four bowls; top evenly with apple mixture and cranberries.   *Makes 4 servings*

Nutrients per Serving (¾ cup oatmeal, ⅓ cup apple mixture and 1 tablespoon cranberries per serving): Calories: 230, Total Fat: 4g, Saturated Fat: 1g, Cholesterol: 3mg, Sodium: 158mg, Carbohydrate: 47g, Fiber: 6g, Protein: 6g

sausage and red pepper strata

Nonstick cooking spray

4 slices day-old French bread, cut into ½-inch pieces

6 ounces bulk reduced-fat breakfast pork sausage

½ teaspoon dried oregano

¼ teaspoon red pepper flakes (optional)

½ medium red bell pepper, finely chopped

¼ cup chopped fresh parsley

1 cup cholesterol-free egg substitute

1 cup evaporated skimmed milk

1 teaspoon Dijon mustard

¼ teaspoon black pepper

½ cup (2 ounces) shredded reduced-fat sharp Cheddar cheese

Additional chopped parsley (optional)

1. Spray 8-inch square baking dish with cooking spray. Line bottom of dish with bread.

2. Spray large nonstick skillet with cooking spray; heat over medium-high heat. Add sausage, oregano and red pepper flakes, if desired; cook and stir 6 to 8 minutes or until sausage is browned, stirring to break up meat. Drain fat. Sprinkle sausage evenly over bread; top with bell pepper and ¼ cup parsley.

3. Whisk egg substitute, milk, mustard and black pepper in medium bowl until well blended. Pour egg mixture over sausage. Cover tightly with foil; refrigerate at least 8 hours or overnight.

4. Preheat oven to 350°F. Bake, covered, 55 minutes.

5. Remove foil. Sprinkle with cheese; bake 5 minutes or until cheese is melted. Garnish with additional parsley. Cut into four pieces before serving.   *Makes 4 servings*

Nutrients per Serving (1 piece): Calories: 298, Total Fat: 12g, Saturated Fat: 2g, Cholesterol: 43mg, Sodium: 719mg, Carbohydrate: 23g, Fiber: 1g, Protein: 25g

sausage and red pepper strata

orange-walnut bread

1¾ cups all-purpose flour

½ cup plus 1 tablespoon sugar, divided

1 tablespoon grated orange peel

1½ teaspoons baking powder

¼ teaspoon baking soda

¼ teaspoon salt

1 egg

¾ cup low-fat buttermilk

⅓ cup plus 2 tablespoons orange juice, divided

¼ cup vegetable oil

½ cup chopped walnuts

1. Preheat oven to 350°F. Grease 8×4-inch loaf pan.

2. Combine flour, ½ cup sugar, orange peel, baking powder, baking soda and salt in medium bowl; mix well. Whisk egg, buttermilk, ⅓ cup orange juice and oil in small bowl until well blended. Add egg mixture to flour mixture; stir just until moistened. Stir in walnuts. Pour into prepared pan.

3. Bake 50 to 55 minutes or until toothpick inserted into center comes out clean.

4. Whisk remaining 2 tablespoons orange juice and 1 tablespoon sugar in small bowl or cup until sugar is dissolved; brush over warm bread. Cool in pan on wire rack 10 minutes. Remove to wire rack; cool completely.

Makes 12 servings

Nutrients per Serving (1 slice): Calories: 191, Total Fat: 9g, Saturated Fat: 1g, Cholesterol: 18mg, Sodium: 158mg, Carbohydrate: 26g, Fiber: 1g, Protein: 4g

orange-walnut bread

whole grain french toast

½ cup egg substitute *or* **2 egg whites**

¼ cup low-fat (1%) milk

½ teaspoon ground cinnamon

¼ teaspoon ground nutmeg

4 teaspoons butter

8 slices 100% whole wheat or multigrain bread

⅓ cup pure maple syrup

1 cup fresh blueberries

2 teaspoons powdered sugar

1. Preheat oven to 400°F. Spray baking sheet with nonstick cooking spray.

2. Whisk egg substitute, milk, cinnamon and nutmeg in shallow bowl until well blended. Melt 1 teaspoon butter in large nonstick skillet over medium heat. Working with two slices at a time, dip each bread slice in milk mixture, turning to coat both sides; let excess mixture drip back into bowl. Cook 2 minutes per side or until golden brown. Transfer to prepared baking sheet. Repeat with remaining butter, bread and milk mixture.

3. Bake 5 to 6 minutes or until heated through.

4. Microwave maple syrup in small microwavable bowl on HIGH 30 seconds or until bubbly. Stir in blueberries. Place french toast on four serving plates; top evenly with blueberry mixture. Sprinkle with powdered sugar.

Makes 4 servings

Nutrients per Serving (2 slices french toast and ¼ cup blueberry mixture):
Calories: 251, Total Fat: 6g, Saturated Fat: 3g, Cholesterol: 11mg, Sodium: 324mg, Carbohydrate: 46g, Fiber: 5g, Protein: 12g

whole grain french toast

english muffin breakfast sandwiches

2 tablespoons plain nonfat yogurt

1 tablespoon spicy brown or Dijon mustard

½ teaspoon dried tarragon or basil

2 English muffins, split and toasted

4 slices Canadian bacon

4 large tomato slices (about ¼ inch thick)

2 slices (1 ounce each) reduced-fat Swiss cheese, cut in half

4 poached eggs (See Tip)

Paprika (optional)

1. Preheat broiler.

2. Stir yogurt, mustard and tarragon in small bowl until well blended. Spread one fourth of yogurt mixture over each muffin half. Top evenly with Canadian bacon, tomato and cheese. Place on broiler pan.

3. Broil 4 inches from heat source 1 minute or until cheese just begins to brown. Top with poached eggs. Sprinkle with paprika, if desired.

Makes 4 servings

Nutrients per Serving (1 topped muffin half): Calories: 233, Total Fat: 9g, Saturated Fat: 3g, Cholesterol: 233mg, Sodium: 836mg, Carbohydrate: 17g, Fiber: 1g, Protein: 18g

Tip: To poach eggs, fill medium saucepan with about 1 quart water; bring to a boil over high heat. Add 2 tablespoons white vinegar and ½ teaspoon salt. Reduce heat to a simmer. Working with one egg at a time, crack egg into small bowl. Gently drop egg into simmering water. (Use a wooden spoon to budge egg gently to keep from sticking to bottom of saucepan.) Simmer 2 to 3 minutes or until white of egg is cooked through. Remove poached egg using slotted spoon. Repeat with remaining eggs.

english muffin breakfast sandwich

cinnamon fruit crunch

1 tablespoon butter

2 tablespoons plus 1 teaspoon packed brown sugar, divided

2¼ teaspoons ground cinnamon, divided

1 cup low-fat granola cereal

¼ cup sliced almonds, toasted*

½ cup vanilla nonfat yogurt

⅛ teaspoon ground nutmeg

2 cans (16 ounces each) mixed fruit chunks in juice, drained

To toast almonds, spread in single layer in heavy-bottomed skillet. Cook over medium heat 1 to 2 minutes, stirring frequently, until lightly browned. Remove from skillet immediately. Cool before using.

1. Melt butter in small saucepan over medium heat. Remove from heat; stir in 2 tablespoons brown sugar and 2 teaspoons cinnamon. Stir in granola and almonds; cool completely.

2. Stir yogurt, remaining 1 teaspoon brown sugar, ¼ teaspoon cinnamon and nutmeg in small bowl until well blended.

3. Spoon about ½ cup mixed fruit into each serving bowl. Top evenly with yogurt mixture; sprinkle with granola mixture.   *Makes 6 servings*

Nutrients per Serving (about ½ cup fruit with 1 tablespoon yogurt mixture and 2 tablespoons granola mixture): Calories: 259, Total Fat: 6g, Saturated Fat: 1g, Cholesterol: 1mg, Sodium: 109mg, Carbohydrate: 48g, Fiber: 6g, Protein: 4g

cinnamon fruit crunch

easy brunch frittata

Nonstick cooking spray
1 cup broccoli, chopped
2½ cups (12 ounces) frozen hash brown potatoes with onions and peppers (O'Brien style), thawed
1½ cups cholesterol-free egg substitute
2 tablespoons reduced-fat (2%) milk
¾ teaspoon salt
¼ teaspoon black pepper
½ cup (2 ounces) shredded reduced-fat Cheddar cheese
Sour cream (optional)

1. Preheat oven to 450°F.

2. Spray medium nonstick ovenproof skillet with cooking spray; heat over medium heat. Add broccoli; cook and stir 2 minutes. Add potatoes; cook and stir 5 minutes.

3. Whisk egg substitute, milk, salt and pepper in small bowl until well blended. Pour egg mixture over potato mixture; cook 5 minutes or until edge is set (center will still be wet).

4. Bake 6 minutes or until center is set. Sprinkle with cheese; let stand 2 to 3 minutes or until cheese is melted.

5. To serve, cut into six wedges; top each wedge with sour cream, if desired.   *Makes 6 servings*

Nutrients per Serving (1 wedge): Calories: 102, Total Fat: 2g, Saturated Fat: 1g, Cholesterol: 7mg, Sodium: 627mg, Carbohydrate: 11g, Fiber: 1g, Protein: 9g

easy brunch frittata

scrambled egg and red pepper pockets

1 egg
2 egg whites
1 tablespoon fat-free (skim) milk
⅛ teaspoon salt (optional)
⅛ teaspoon black pepper
1½ teaspoons unsalted butter, softened and divided
3 tablespoons minced red onion
2 tablespoons diced jarred roasted red pepper, drained
1 whole wheat pita bread round, cut in half crosswise

1. Whisk egg, egg whites, milk, salt, if desired, and black pepper in small bowl until well blended.

2. Spray medium skillet with nonstick cooking spray. Add ½ teaspoon butter; heat over medium heat. Add onion; cook and stir 3 to 5 minutes or until lightly browned. Pour egg mixture into skillet; sprinkle with red peppers. Stir gently, lifting edge to allow uncooked portion to flow underneath. Continue cooking until set.

3. Evenly spread inside of each pita half with remaining 1 teaspoon butter. Spoon egg mixture into pita halves. *Makes 2 servings*

Nutrients per Serving (1 filled pita half): Calories: 155, Total Fat: 6g, Saturated Fat: 3g, Cholesterol: 113mg, Sodium: 285mg, Carbohydrate: 17g, Fiber: 3g, Protein: 8g

Note: An ideal breakfast includes lean protein, complex carbohydrates, and a little bit of fat. This recipe includes all of the important aspects for a nutritious meal; it's filling enough to get you through the morning.

scrambled egg and red pepper pocket

raspberry white chocolate danishes

1 package (8 ounces) refrigerated reduced-fat crescent roll dough
8 teaspoons no-sugar-added red raspberry preserves
1 square (1 ounce) white chocolate, chopped

1. Preheat oven to 375°F. Spray baking sheet with nonstick cooking spray.

2. Unroll crescent dough and separate into 8 triangles. Place 1 teaspoon preserves in center of each triangle. Fold right and left corners of long side over filling to top corner to form rectangle. Pinch edges to seal. Place seam side up on prepared baking sheet.

3. Bake 12 minutes or until lightly browned. Remove to wire rack; cool 5 minutes.

4. Place white chocolate in small resealable food storage bag. Microwave on MEDIUM (50%) 1 minute; gently knead bag. Microwave and knead at additional 30-second intervals until white chocolate is completely melted. Cut off tiny corner of bag; drizzle white chocolate over danishes.   *Makes 8 danishes*

Nutrients per Serving (1 danish): Calories: 115, Total Fat: 6g, Saturated Fat: 3g, Cholesterol: 1mg, Sodium: 227mg, Carbohydrate: 16g, Fiber: 0g, Protein: 2g

whoa breakfast

3 cups water
2 cups chopped peeled apples
1½ cups steel-cut or old-fashioned oats
¼ cup sliced almonds
½ teaspoon ground cinnamon

Slow Cooker Directions

Combine water, apples, oats, almonds and cinnamon in slow cooker. Cover; cook on LOW 8 hours.   *Makes 6 servings*

Nutrients per Serving (about ½ cup): Calories: 119, Total Fat: 3g, Saturated Fat: <1g, Cholesterol: 0mg, Sodium: <1mg, Carbohydrate: 20g, Fiber: 4g, Protein: 3g

raspberry white chocolate danishes

oatmeal banana pancakes

1⅓ cups fat-free (skim) milk

½ cup quick oats

1 cup all-purpose flour

2 teaspoons baking powder

1 egg, beaten

2 teaspoons canola oil

1 large banana, peeled and mashed

½ cup sugar-free strawberry preserves

1. Combine milk and oats in large bowl; let stand 10 minutes.

2. Sift flour and baking powder into medium bowl. Add flour mixture, egg and oil to oat mixture; stir until moistened. Stir in banana.

3. Heat large griddle coated with nonstick cooking spray over medium heat. Drop ¼ cupfuls batter onto griddle; cook 2 to 3 minutes or until bubbles form on top and bottoms are golden brown. Turn over; cook 1 to 2 minutes or until golden brown.

4. Microwave preserves in small microwavable bowl on HIGH 1 minute or until heated through. Place 3 pancakes on each serving plate; top with 2 tablespoons preserves. *Makes 6 servings*

Nutrients per Serving (3 pancakes and 2 tablespoons preserves):
Calories: 176, Total Fat: 3g, Saturated Fat: 1g, Cholesterol: 36mg, Sodium: 198mg, Carbohydrate: 35g, Fiber: 2g, Protein: 6g

oatmeal banana pancakes

greek isles omelet

Nonstick cooking spray
¼ **cup chopped onion**
¼ **cup canned artichoke hearts, rinsed and drained**
¼ **cup chopped spinach**
¼ **cup chopped plum tomato**
2 **tablespoons sliced pitted ripe olives, rinsed and drained**
1 **cup cholesterol-free egg substitute**
Dash black pepper

1. Spray small nonstick skillet with cooking spray; heat over medium heat. Add onion; cook and stir 2 minutes or until crisp-tender. Add artichokes; cook and stir until heated through. Add spinach, tomato and olives; gently stir. Remove to small bowl.

2. Wipe out skillet with paper towels and spray with cooking spray. Whisk egg substitute and pepper in medium bowl until well blended. Heat skillet over medium heat. Pour egg mixture into skillet; cook and stir gently, lifting edge to allow uncooked portion to flow underneath. Continue cooking until set.

3. Spoon vegetable mixture over half of omelet; gently loosen omelet with spatula and fold in half. Serve immediately.   *Makes 2 servings*

Nutrients per Serving (½ of omelet): Calories: 111, Total Fat: 3g, Saturated Fat: <1g, Cholesterol: 0mg, Sodium: 538mg, Carbohydrate: 7g, Fiber: 1g, Protein: 13g

greek isles omelet

whole wheat pumpkin muffins

1½ cups whole wheat flour
¼ cup sugar
1 teaspoon salt
1 teaspoon ground allspice
1 teaspoon ground nutmeg
¾ teaspoon baking powder
½ teaspoon baking soda
¾ cup canned pumpkin
½ cup canola oil
½ cup honey
½ cup frozen apple juice concentrate, thawed
½ cup chopped walnuts
½ cup golden raisins

1. Preheat oven to 350°F. Spray 12 standard (2½-inch) muffin cups with nonstick cooking spray.

2. Combine flour, sugar, salt, allspice, nutmeg, baking powder and baking soda in large bowl; mix well. Stir in pumpkin, oil, honey and apple juice until well blended. Stir in walnuts and raisins. Spoon evenly into prepared muffin cups.

3. Bake 12 to 15 minutes or until toothpick inserted into centers comes out clean. Remove to wire rack; cool completely. *Makes 12 muffins*

Nutrients per Serving (1 muffin): Calories: 268, Total Fat: 12g, Saturated Fat: 1g, Cholesterol: 0mg, Sodium: 283mg, Carbohydrate: 39g, Fiber: 3g, Protein: 3g

whole wheat pumpkin muffins

ham & egg breakfast panini

Nonstick cooking spray

¼ **cup chopped green or red bell pepper**

2 **tablespoons sliced green onion**

1 **slice (1 ounce) reduced-fat smoked deli ham, chopped**

½ **cup cholesterol-free egg substitute**

Black pepper

4 **slices multigrain or whole grain bread**

2 **slices (¾-ounce each) reduced-fat Cheddar or Swiss cheese**

1. Spray small skillet with cooking spray; heat over medium heat. Add bell pepper and green onion; cook and stir 4 minutes or until crisp-tender. Stir in ham.

2. Whisk egg substitute and black pepper in small bowl until well blended. Pour egg mixture into skillet; cook 2 minutes or until egg mixture is almost set, stirring occasionally.

3. Heat grill pan or medium skillet over medium heat. Spray one side of each bread slice with cooking spray; turn bread over. Top each bread slice with 1 cheese slice and half of egg mixture. Top with second bread slice. Repeat with remaining bread slices, cheese slices and egg mixture.

4. Grill 2 minutes per side, pressing down lightly with spatula until toasted. (Cover pan with lid during last 2 minutes of cooking to melt cheese, if desired.) Serve immediately. *Makes 2 sandwiches*

Nutrients per Serving (1 sandwich): Calories: 271, Total Fat: 5g, Saturated Fat: 1g, Cholesterol: 9mg, Sodium: 577mg, Carbohydrate: 30g, Fiber: 6g, Protein: 24g

ham & egg breakfast panini

apricot-cherry coffee cake

1½ **cups all-purpose flour**

½ **cup packed brown sugar**

1 **teaspoon ground cinnamon**

½ **teaspoon baking powder**

¼ **teaspoon baking soda**

¼ **teaspoon salt**

¾ **cup low-fat buttermilk**

¼ **cup (½ stick) butter, melted**

1 **egg**

1½ **teaspoons vanilla**

⅓ **cup chopped dried tart cherries**

⅓ **cup finely chopped dried apricots**

3 **tablespoons flaked coconut**

1. Preheat oven to 350°F. Spray 8-inch round baking pan with nonstick cooking spray.

2. Combine flour, brown sugar, cinnamon, baking powder, baking soda and salt in large bowl; mix well. Whisk buttermilk, butter, egg and vanilla in small bowl until well blended. Stir in cherries and apricots. Stir egg mixture into flour mixture just until blended. Pour into prepared pan. Sprinkle with coconut.

3. Bake 25 minutes or until toothpick inserted into center comes out clean. Cool in pan on wire rack 10 minutes. Cut into wedges. Serve warm.   *Makes 10 servings*

Nutrients per Serving (1 wedge): Calories: 199, Total Fat: 6g, Saturated Fat: 4g, Cholesterol: 34mg, Sodium: 179mg, Carbohydrate: 33g, Fiber: 1g, Protein: 4g

apricot-cherry coffee cake

mexican breakfast burrito

1 container (16 ounces) cholesterol-free egg substitute
⅛ teaspoon black pepper
  Nonstick cooking spray
⅓ cup canned black beans, rinsed and drained
2 tablespoons sliced green onion
2 (10-inch) flour tortillas
3 tablespoons shredded reduced-fat Cheddar cheese
3 tablespoons salsa

1. Whisk egg substitute and pepper in medium bowl until well blended. Spray large nonstick skillet with cooking spray; heat over medium heat. Pour egg mixture into skillet; cook 5 to 7 minutes or until mixture begins to set, stirring occasionally. Stir in beans and green onion; cook and stir 3 minutes or just until cooked through.

2. Spoon mixture evenly down centers of tortillas; top evenly with cheese. Roll up to enclose filling. Cut in half; top with salsa.   *Makes 4 servings*

Nutrients per Serving (½ of burrito): Calories: 200, Total Fat: 4g, Saturated Fat: 1g, Cholesterol: 5mg, Sodium: 590mg, Carbohydrate: 22g, Fiber: 5g, Protein: 17g

tropical parfait

1½ cups orange or vanilla nonfat yogurt
1 can (11 ounces) mandarin oranges in light syrup, drained and chopped
1 can (8 ounces) pineapple chunks in juice, drained
1 medium banana, sliced
2 tablespoons shredded coconut

1. Combine yogurt and oranges in medium bowl.

2. Spoon half of yogurt mixture into four serving bowls. Top evenly with pineapple. Spoon remaining half of yogurt mixture over pineapple. Top evenly with banana slices. Sprinkle with coconut. Serve immediately.
Makes 4 servings

Nutrients per Serving (1 parfait): Calories: 170, Total Fat: 1g, Saturated Fat: 1g, Cholesterol: 0mg, Sodium: 60mg, Carbohydrate: 40g, Fiber: 2g, Protein: 4g

mexican breakfast burrito

cranberry scones

1½ **cups all-purpose flour**

½ **cup oat bran**

¼ **cup plus 1 tablespoon sugar, divided**

2 **teaspoons baking powder**

½ **teaspoon baking soda**

½ **teaspoon salt**

¼ **cup (½ stick) plus 1 tablespoon cold margarine or butter**

¾ **cup dried cranberries**

⅓ **cup fat-free (skim) milk**

1 **egg**

¼ **cup sour cream**

1 **tablespoon old-fashioned or quick oats (optional)**

1. Preheat oven to 425°F.

2. Combine flour, oat bran, ¼ cup sugar, baking powder, baking soda and salt in large bowl; mix well. Cut in margarine with pastry blender or two knives until mixture resembles coarse crumbs. Stir in cranberries.

3. Whisk milk and egg in small bowl until well blended. Reserve 2 tablespoons milk mixture. Stir sour cream into remaining milk mixture. Stir into flour mixture until soft dough forms.

4. Turn out dough onto floured surface. Gently knead 10 to 12 times. Shape dough into 9×6-inch rectangle. Cut dough into six 3-inch squares, using floured knife; cut diagonally into halves, forming 12 triangles. Place 2 inches apart on ungreased baking sheets; brush with reserved milk mixture. Sprinkle with oats, if desired, and remaining 1 tablespoon sugar.

5. Bake 10 to 12 minutes or until golden brown. Remove to wire rack; cool 10 minutes. Serve warm. *Makes 12 scones*

Nutrients per Serving (1 scone): Calories: 160, Total Fat: 5g, Saturated Fat: 2g, Cholesterol: 20mg, Sodium: 280mg, Carbohydrate: 27g, Fiber: 1g, Protein: 3g

cranberry scones

Snacks
& Starters

wild wedges

- 2 (8-inch) fat-free flour tortillas
  Nonstick cooking spray
- ⅓ cup shredded reduced-fat Cheddar cheese
- ⅓ cup chopped cooked chicken or turkey
- 1 green onion, thinly sliced
- 2 tablespoons mild thick and chunky salsa

Heat large nonstick skillet over medium heat. Spray one side of 1 tortilla with cooking spray; place in skillet, sprayed side down. Top with cheese, chicken, green onion and salsa. Place remaining tortilla on top; spray with cooking spray. Cook 2 to 3 minutes per side or until golden brown and cheese is melted. To serve, cut into eight wedges.

Makes 4 servings

Nutrients per Serving (2 wedges): Calories: 82, Total Fat: 2g, Saturated Fat: 1g, Cholesterol: 13mg, Sodium: 224mg, Carbohydrate: 8g, Fiber: 3g, Protein: 7g

Variation: For bean quesadillas, omit the chicken and spread ⅓ cup canned fat-free refried beans over one of the tortillas.

herbed stuffed tomatoes

15 cherry tomatoes
½ cup low-fat (1%) cottage cheese
1 tablespoon thinly sliced green onion
1 teaspoon chopped fresh chervil *or* ¼ teaspoon dried chervil
½ teaspoon snipped fresh dill *or* ⅛ teaspoon dried dill weed
⅛ teaspoon lemon pepper

1. Cut thin slice off bottom of each tomato. Scoop out pulp with small spoon; discard pulp. Invert tomatoes onto paper towels to drain.

2. Stir cottage cheese, green onion, chervil, dill and lemon pepper in small bowl until just combined. Spoon evenly into tomatoes. Serve immediately or cover and refrigerate up to 8 hours.   *Makes 5 servings*

Nutrients per Serving (3 stuffed tomatoes): Calories: 27, Total Fat: <1g, Saturated Fat: <1g, Cholesterol: 1mg, Sodium: 96mg, Carbohydrate: 3g, Fiber: <1g, Protein: 3g

crunchy-fruity snack mix

1 cup (4 ounces) roasted and salted soy nuts
1 cup broken-in-half pretzel sticks (about 1½ ounces)
⅔ cup dried cranberries
⅔ cup dried pineapple, cut into ½-inch pieces
⅔ cup white chocolate chips

Combine soy nuts, pretzel sticks, cranberries, pineapple and white chocolate chips in large bowl; mix well. Store in airtight container.
Makes 16 servings

Nutrients per Serving (¹⁄₁₆ of total recipe): Calories: 110, Total Fat: 4g, Saturated Fat: 2g, Cholesterol: 0mg, Sodium: 60mg, Carbohydrate: 17g, Fiber: 1g, Protein: 3g

Serving Suggestions: For breakfast, try Crunchy-Fruity Snack Mix on hot or cold cereal or sprinkle it on waffles or pancakes. Or for dessert, use it as an ice cream topper or mix it into cookie doughs or muffin and quick bread batters.

herbed stuffed tomatoes

bell pepper nachos

Nonstick cooking spray
1 medium green bell pepper
1 medium yellow or red bell pepper
2 Italian plum tomatoes, seeded and finely chopped
⅓ cup finely chopped onion
1 teaspoon chili powder
½ teaspoon ground cumin
1½ cups cooked white rice
½ cup (2 ounces) shredded reduced-fat Monterey Jack cheese
¼ cup chopped fresh cilantro
2 teaspoons jalapeño pepper sauce *or* ¼ teaspoon hot pepper sauce
½ cup (2 ounces) shredded reduced-fat sharp Cheddar cheese

1. Spray baking sheets with cooking spray. Cut bell peppers into bite-size triangles; set aside.

2. Spray large nonstick skillet with cooking spray. Add tomatoes, onion, chili powder and cumin; cook and stir over medium heat 3 minutes or until onion is tender. Remove from heat. Stir in rice, Monterey Jack cheese, cilantro and jalapeño pepper sauce.

3. Top each pepper triangle with about 2 tablespoons rice mixture; sprinkle with Cheddar cheese. Place on prepared baking sheets; cover and refrigerate 1 hour or up to 8 hours.

4. Preheat broiler. Broil nachos 6 to 8 inches from heat source 3 to 4 minutes or until cheese is bubbly and rice is heated through.

Makes 8 servings

Nutrients per Serving (4 nachos): Calories: 100, Total Fat: 3g, Saturated Fat: 1g, Cholesterol: 14mg, Sodium: 165mg, Carbohydrate: 14g, Fiber: 1g, Protein: 6g

bell pepper nachos

apricot chicken pot stickers

Sweet and Sour Sauce (page 44)
2 cups plus 1 tablespoon water, divided
2 boneless skinless chicken breasts (about 8 ounces)
2 cups chopped finely shredded cabbage
½ cup apricot fruit spread
2 green onions, finely chopped
2 teaspoons reduced-sodium soy sauce
½ teaspoon grated fresh ginger
⅛ teaspoon black pepper
30 (3-inch) wonton wrappers
Shredded or matchstick carrots (optional)

1. Prepare Sweet and Sour Sauce; set aside.

2. Bring 2 cups water to a boil in medium saucepan. Add chicken. Reduce heat to low; cover and simmer 10 minutes or until chicken is cooked through (165°F). Drain; set aside.

3. Combine cabbage and remaining 1 tablespoon water in same saucepan; cook over high heat 1 to 2 minutes or until water is evaporated, stirring occasionally. Remove from heat; cool slightly.

4. Finely chop chicken. Return chicken to saucepan. Add fruit spread, green onions, soy sauce, ginger and pepper; mix well.

5. Working with one at a time, spoon slightly rounded tablespoonful chicken mixture into center of 1 wonton wrapper; brush edges with water. Bring four corners to center; press to seal. Repeat with remaining wrappers and filling.

6. Spray steamer basket with nonstick cooking spray. Place in wok or large saucepan. Add water to ½ inch below steamer. (Water should not touch steamer.) Remove steamer. Cover wok; bring to a boil over high heat. Fill steamer with pot stickers, leaving space between so pot stickers do not touch. Carefully place steamer in wok. Steam, covered, 5 minutes. Transfer to serving plate. Repeat with remaining pot stickers, if necessary. Serve with Sweet and Sour Sauce.   *Makes 10 servings*

Nutrients per Serving (3 pot stickers): Calories: 145, Total Fat: 1g, Saturated Fat: <1g, Cholesterol: 17mg, Sodium: 223mg, Carbohydrate: 26g, Fiber: 1g, Protein: 8g

continued on page 44

apricot chicken pot stickers

apricot chicken pot stickers, continued

sweet and sour sauce

1 cup apricot fruit spread or preserves
¼ cup cider or white vinegar
2 tablespoons brown sugar
½ to 1 teaspoon dry mustard
½ teaspoon ground ginger

Combine fruit spread, vinegar, brown sugar, mustard and ginger in small saucepan; cook and stir over low heat until sugar is melted; remove from heat. Cool completely.

cheesy potato skins

2 tablespoons grated Parmesan cheese
3 cloves garlic, finely chopped
2 teaspoons dried rosemary
½ teaspoon salt
¼ teaspoon black pepper
4 baked potatoes
2 egg whites, lightly beaten
½ cup (2 ounces) shredded part-skim mozzarella cheese
   Salsa (optional)

1. Preheat oven to 400°F. Combine Parmesan cheese, garlic, rosemary, salt and pepper in small bowl; mix well.

2. Cut potatoes lengthwise in half. Remove and discard pulp, leaving ¼-inch-thick shells. Cut each potato half lengthwise into two wedges. Place on baking sheet.

3. Brush potato wedges with egg whites; sprinkle with Parmesan cheese mixture. Bake 20 minutes.

4. Sprinkle with mozzarella cheese. Bake 2 minutes or until cheese is melted. Serve with salsa, if desired.   *Makes 8 servings*

Nutrients per Serving (2 potato skins): Calories: 90, Total Fat: 2g, Saturated Fat: 1g, Cholesterol: 5mg, Sodium: 215mg, Carbohydrate: 14g, Fiber: 2g, Protein: 5g

falafel nuggets

Falafel

- 2 cans (about 15 ounces each) chickpeas
- ½ cup whole wheat flour
- ½ cup chopped fresh parsley
- ⅓ cup lemon juice
- ¼ cup minced onion
- 2 tablespoons minced garlic
- 2 teaspoons ground cumin
- ½ teaspoon salt
- ½ teaspoon ground red pepper or red pepper flakes
- ½ cup canola oil

Sauce

- 2½ cups tomato sauce
- ⅓ cup tomato paste
- 2 tablespoons lemon juice
- 2 teaspoons sugar
- 1 teaspoon onion powder
- ½ teaspoon salt

1. Preheat oven to 400°F. Spray baking sheet with nonstick cooking spray.

2. Drain chickpeas, reserving ¼ cup liquid. Combine chickpeas, reserved ¼ cup liquid, flour, parsley, ⅓ cup lemon juice, minced onion, garlic, cumin, ½ teaspoon salt and red pepper in food processor or blender; process until well blended. Shape into 36 (1-inch) balls; place 1 to 2 inches apart on prepared baking sheet. Refrigerate 15 minutes.

3. Meanwhile, combine tomato sauce, tomato paste, 2 tablespoons lemon juice, sugar, onion powder and ½ teaspoon salt in medium saucepan. Simmer over medium-low heat 20 minutes; keep warm.

4. Heat oil in large nonstick skillet over medium-high heat to 350°F. Fry falafel in batches until browned. Place on baking sheet; bake 8 to 10 minutes. Serve with warm sauce. *Makes 12 servings*

Nutrients per Serving (3 falafel nuggets with ¼ cup sauce): Calories: 191, Total Fat: 7g, Saturated Fat: 1g, Cholesterol: 0mg, Sodium: 701mg, Carbohydrate: 26g, Fiber: 5g, Protein: 6g

Note: Falafel also can be baked completely to reduce fat content. Spray balls lightly with nonstick cooking spray and bake on baking sheet 15 to 20 minutes, turning once.

savory pita chips

2 whole wheat or white pita bread rounds
   Olive oil cooking spray
3 tablespoons grated Parmesan cheese
 1 teaspoon dried basil
¼ teaspoon garlic powder

1. Preheat oven to 350°F. Line baking sheet with foil.

2. Carefully cut each pita horizontally to split and form two rounds. Cut each round into six wedges.

3. Place wedges, inside layer down, on prepared baking sheet. Spray with cooking spray. Turn over; spray again.

4. Combine cheese, basil and garlic powder in small bowl; mix well. Sprinkle evenly over pita wedges.

5. Bake 12 to 14 minutes or until golden brown. Cool completely.

Makes 4 servings

Nutrients per Serving (6 pita chips): Calories: 108, Total Fat: 2g, Saturated Fat: 1g, Cholesterol: 4mg, Sodium: 257mg, Carbohydrate: 18g, Fiber: 2g, Protein: 5g

Cinnamon Crisps: Substitute butter-flavored cooking spray for olive oil cooking spray and 1 tablespoon sugar mixed with ¼ teaspoon ground cinnamon for Parmesan cheese, basil and garlic powder.

savory pita chips

roasted garlic spread with three cheeses

2 medium heads garlic
2 packages (8 ounces each) fat-free cream cheese, softened
1 package (3½ ounces) goat cheese
2 tablespoons (1 ounce) crumbled blue cheese, plus additional for garnish
1 teaspoon dried thyme
Assorted sliced fresh vegetables
Fresh thyme (optional)

1. Preheat oven to 400°F. Cut tops off garlic heads to expose tops of cloves. Place garlic in small baking pan. Bake 45 minutes or until very tender. Remove from pan; cool completely. Squeeze garlic into small bowl; mash with fork. Discard skins.

2. Beat cream cheese and goat cheese in small bowl until smooth; stir in garlic, 2 tablespoons blue cheese and 1 teaspoon dried thyme. Cover and refrigerate 3 hours or overnight.

3. Spoon dip into serving bowl; serve with fresh vegetables. Garnish with additional blue cheese and fresh thyme.   *Makes about 20 servings*

Nutrients per Serving (2 tablespoons): Calories: 37, Total Fat: 1g, Saturated Fat: <1g, Cholesterol: 9mg, Sodium: 157mg, Carbohydrate: 2g, Fiber: <1g, Protein: 4g

roasted garlic spread with three cheeses

caponata

1 medium eggplant (about 1 pound), peeled and cut into
   ½-inch pieces

1 can (about 14 ounces) diced Italian plum tomatoes

1 onion, chopped

1 red bell pepper, cut into ½-inch pieces

½ cup salsa

¼ cup olive oil

2 tablespoons capers, drained

2 tablespoons balsamic vinegar

3 cloves garlic, minced

1 teaspoon dried oregano

¼ teaspoon salt

⅓ cup packed fresh basil, cut into thin strips

   Toasted Italian or French bread slices (optional)

Slow Cooker Directions

1. Combine eggplant, tomatoes, onion, bell pepper, salsa, oil, capers, vinegar, garlic, oregano and salt in slow cooker. Cover; cook on LOW 7 to 8 hours.

2. Stir in basil. Serve at room temperature on bread slices, if desired.

Makes about 5¼ cups

Nutrients per Serving (2 tablespoons): Calories: 42, Total Fat: 3g, Saturated Fat: 0g, Cholesterol: 0mg, Sodium: 141mg, Carbohydrate: 4g, Fiber: <1g, Protein: <1g

caponata

guiltless cocktail shrimp

Nonstick cooking spray
1 pound medium raw shrimp peeled and deveined
¼ teaspoon salt
¼ teaspoon black pepper
¼ teaspoon ground red pepper, divided (optional)
½ cup ketchup
1 to 2 tablespoons prepared horseradish
1½ teaspoons lemon juice
1 teaspoon Worcestershire sauce
⅛ teaspoon hot pepper sauce
Lemon wedges (optional)

1. Heat large nonstick skillet over medium heat; spray with cooking spray. Add shrimp; season with salt, black pepper and ⅛ teaspoon red pepper, if desired. Cook 5 to 6 minutes or until shrimp are pink and opaque, stirring frequently. Remove from heat; drain well. Cool completely.

2. Stir ketchup, horseradish, lemon juice, Worcestershire sauce, remaining ⅛ teaspoon red pepper, if desired, and hot pepper sauce in small bowl until well blended.

3. Serve shrimp with cocktail sauce and lemon wedges, if desired.

Makes 6 servings

Nutrients per Serving (⅓ cup shrimp with 2 tablespoons sauce):
Calories: 103, Total Fat: 1g, Saturated Fat: <1g, Cholesterol: 115mg,
Sodium: 483mg, Carbohydrate: 7g, Fiber: <1g, Protein: 15g

guiltless cocktail shrimp

spinach quiches

1 package (15 ounces) refrigerated pie crusts

2 teaspoons vegetable oil

¼ cup finely chopped mushrooms

2 tablespoons finely chopped onion

1 clove garlic, minced

1 cup frozen chopped spinach, thawed and squeezed dry

1 teaspoon dried oregano

½ teaspoon dried mint

½ cup whole-milk ricotta cheese

2 eggs

2 tablespoons all-purpose flour

2 tablespoons reduced-fat (2%) milk

¾ teaspoon salt

⅛ teaspoon ground white pepper

1. Preheat oven to 400°F. Roll out one pie crust to ⅛-inch thickness on floured surface. Cut out 12 circles with 2½-inch biscuit or round cookie cutter. Repeat with remaining pie crust.

2. Line 24 mini (1¾-inch) muffin cups with cutouts. Bake 8 to 10 minutes or until lightly browned. Cool in pans 10 minutes.

3. *Reduce oven temperature to 325°F.* Heat oil in medium saucepan over medium heat. Add mushrooms, onion and garlic; cook and stir 2 minutes or until onion is tender. Stir in spinach, oregano and mint; cook and stir 5 minutes or until liquid is evaporated. Remove from heat; stir in ricotta cheese, eggs, flour, milk, salt and white pepper until well blended. Spoon 2 teaspoons mixture into each prepared muffin cup.

4. Bake 20 minutes or until set and tops are lightly browned. Cool in pans on wire racks 10 minutes before serving. *Makes 24 servings*

Nutrients per Serving (1 quiche): Calories: 80, Total Fat: 4g, Saturated Fat: 2g, Cholesterol: 20mg, Sodium: 150mg, Carbohydrate: 7g, Fiber: 0g, Protein: 2g

Note: Refrigerate prebaked quiches, covered, up to 1 day or freeze them up to 1 month. To serve, preheat oven to 325°F. Bake 10 minutes or until heated through. (If frozen, thaw overnight in refrigerator.)

spinach quiches

whole grain cereal bars

5 to 6 cups assorted whole grain cereals
1 package (10 ounces) large marshmallows
¼ cup (½ stick) butter
¼ cup old-fashioned oats

1. Grease 13×19-inch baking pan.

2. Place cereals in large resealable food storage bag; seal bag. Using rolling pin, lightly roll over bag until cereals are crumbled.

3. Combine marshmallows and butter in large saucepan over medium-low heat; cook and stir until marshmallows are melted and mixture is smooth. Remove from heat.

4. Stir in cereal until well blended. Using waxed paper, press cereal mixture evenly into prepared pan. Sprinkle with oats. Let stand until firm. Cut into bars. *Makes 24 bars*

Nutrients per Serving (1 bar): Calories: 88, Total Fat: 2g, Saturated Fat: 1g, Cholesterol: 5mg, Sodium: 76mg, Carbohydrate: 17g, Fiber: 1g, Protein: <1g

rosemary-scented nut mix

2 tablespoons unsalted butter
2 cups pecan halves
1 cup macadamia nuts
1 cup walnuts
1 teaspoon dried rosemary
½ teaspoon salt
¼ teaspoon red pepper flakes

1. Preheat oven to 300°F.

2. Melt butter in large saucepan over low heat. Stir in pecans, macadamia nuts and walnuts. Add rosemary, salt and red pepper flakes; cook and stir about 1 minute. Spread mixture onto ungreased baking sheet.

3. Bake 15 minutes, stirring occasionally. Cool completely on baking sheet on wire rack. *Makes 32 servings*

Nutrients per Serving (2 tablespoons): Calories: 108, Total Fat: 11g, Saturated Fat: 2g, Cholesterol: 2mg, Sodium: 37mg, Carbohydrate: 2g, Fiber: 1g, Protein: 2g

whole grain cereal bars

quick and easy stuffed mushrooms

 1 slice whole wheat bread
16 large mushrooms
 ½ cup sliced celery
 ½ cup sliced onion
 1 clove garlic
   Nonstick cooking spray
 1 teaspoon Worcestershire sauce
 ½ teaspoon marjoram leaves, crushed
 ⅛ teaspoon ground red pepper
   Dash paprika

1. Preheat oven to 350°F. Tear bread into pieces; place in food processor. Process 30 seconds or until crumbs are formed. Transfer to small bowl; set aside.

2. Remove stems from mushrooms; reserve caps. Place mushroom stems, celery, onion and garlic in food processor; process using on/off pulsing action until vegetables are finely chopped.

3. Spray large nonstick skillet with cooking spray. Add vegetable mixture; cook and stir over medium heat 5 minutes or until onion is tender. Remove to bowl. Stir in bread crumbs, Worcestershire sauce, marjoram and red pepper.

4. Fill mushroom caps evenly with mixture, pressing down firmly. Place about ½ inch apart in shallow baking pan. Spray tops with cooking spray. Sprinkle with paprika.

5. Bake 15 minutes or until heated through.   *Makes 8 servings*

Nutrients per Serving (2 stuffed mushrooms): Calories: 20, Total Fat: <1g, Saturated Fat: <1g, Cholesterol: 0mg, Sodium: 29mg, Carbohydrate: 4g, Fiber: 1g, Protein: 1g

Note: Mushrooms can be stuffed up to 1 day ahead. Refrigerate filled mushroom caps, covered, until ready to serve. Bake in preheated 300°F oven 20 minutes or until heated through.

quick and easy stuffed mushrooms

bacon & onion cheese ball

1 package (8 ounces) fat-free cream cheese, softened
½ cup fat-free sour cream
½ cup bottled real bacon bits
½ cup chopped green onions, plus additional for garnish
¼ cup (1 ounce) crumbled blue cheese
Celery sticks or whole wheat crackers (optional)

1. Beat cream cheese, sour cream, bacon bits, green onions and blue cheese in large bowl until well blended. Shape mixture into ball. Wrap in plastic wrap; refrigerate at least 1 hour.

2. Place cheese ball on serving plate. Garnish with additional green onions. Serve with celery or crackers, if desired. *Makes 20 servings*

Nutrients per Serving (2 tablespoons): Calories: 34, Total Fat: 1g, Saturated Fat: <1g, Cholesterol: 7mg, Sodium: 203mg, Carbohydrate: 2g, Fiber: <1g, Protein: 4g

warm peanut-caramel dip

¼ cup reduced-fat peanut butter
2 tablespoons fat-free (skim) milk
2 tablespoons fat-free caramel ice cream topping
1 large apple, thinly sliced (24 slices)
4 large pretzel rods, broken in half

1. Combine peanut butter, milk and caramel topping in small saucepan. Heat over low heat until mixture is melted and smooth, stirring constantly.

2. Serve with apple slices and pretzels. *Makes 1¾ cups*

Nutrients per Serving (1½ tablespoons dip with 6 apple slices and 2 pretzel halves): Calories: 189, Total Fat: 6g, Saturated Fat: 1g, Cholesterol: <1mg, Sodium: 282mg, Carbohydrate: 29g, Fiber: 3g, Protein: 5g

Microwave Directions: Combine peanut butter, milk and caramel topping in small microwavable bowl. Microwave on MEDIUM (50%) 1 minute; stir. Microwave at additional 30-second intervals until mixture is melted and smooth.

bacon & onion cheese ball

herb cheese twists

2 tablespoons butter or margarine
¼ cup grated Parmesan cheese
1 teaspoon dried parsley
1 teaspoon dried basil
1 can (about 6 ounces) refrigerated buttermilk biscuits (5 count)

1. Preheat oven to 400°F. Grease baking sheet. Microwave butter in small microwavable bowl on MEDIUM (50%) 1 minute or just until melted; cool slightly. Stir in cheese, parsley and basil.

2. Stretch biscuits into 5×2-inch rectangles. Spread 1 teaspoon butter mixture onto each rectangle. Cut in half lengthwise; twist three or four times. Place on prepared baking sheet.

3. Bake 8 to 10 minutes or until golden brown.   *Makes 10 twists*

Nutrients per Serving (1 twist): Calories: 80, Total Fat: 5g, Saturated Fat: 3g, Cholesterol: 10mg, Sodium: 210mg, Carbohydrate: 7g, Fiber: 0g, Protein: 2g

Variation: Save even more time by using ready-to-bake breadsticks. Spread the butter mixture onto the breadsticks, then bake them according to the package directions.

fruit kabobs with raspberry yogurt dip

½ cup plain nonfat yogurt
¼ cup no-sugar-added raspberry fruit spread
1 pint fresh strawberries
2 cups cubed honeydew melon (1-inch cubes)
2 cups cubed cantaloupe (1-inch cubes)
1 can (8 ounces) pineapple chunks in juice, drained

1. Stir yogurt and fruit spread in small bowl until well blended.

2. Thread fruit alternately onto six 12-inch skewers. Serve with yogurt dip.
                                                                Makes 6 servings

Nutrients per Serving (1 kabob with 2 tablespoons dip): Calories: 108, Total Fat: <1g, Saturated Fat: <1g, Cholesterol: <1mg, Sodium: 52mg, Carbohydrate: 25g, Fiber: 2g, Protein: 2g

herb cheese twists

vegetable-topped hummus

1 can (about 15 ounces) chickpeas, rinsed and drained
2 tablespoons tahini*
2 tablespoons lemon juice
1 clove garlic
¾ teaspoon salt
1 tomato, finely chopped
2 green onions, finely chopped
2 tablespoons chopped fresh parsley
   Pita bread or assorted crackers (optional)

Tahini is a thick paste made of ground sesame seeds that is used in Middle Eastern cooking.

1. Combine chickpeas, tahini, lemon juice, garlic and salt in food processor or blender; process until smooth.

2. Combine tomato, green onions and parsley in small bowl; gently toss to combine.

3. Spoon chickpea mixture into serving bowl; top with tomato mixture. Serve with pita bread or assorted crackers, if desired.

Makes 8 servings

Nutrients per Serving (6 tablespoons): Calories: 82, Total Fat: 3g, Saturated Fat: <1g, Cholesterol: 0mg, Sodium: 429mg, Carbohydrate: 11g, Fiber: 3g, Protein: 3g

quick pizza snacks

3 English muffins, split and toasted
1 can (about 14 ounces) Italian-style diced tomatoes
¾ cup (3 ounces) shredded Italian cheese blend

1. Preheat oven to 350°F.

2. Place muffin halves on ungreased baking sheet. Top each half with ¼ cup tomatoes; sprinkle with 2 tablespoons cheese.

3. Bake 5 minutes or until cheese is melted and lightly browned.

Makes 6 servings

Nutrients per Serving (1 pizza snack): Calories: 155, Total Fat: 5g, Saturated Fat: 2g, Cholesterol: 12mg, Sodium: 557mg, Carbohydrate: 22g, Fiber: 1g, Protein: 8g

vegetable-topped hummus

Main
Dishes

tuscan turkey and white bean skillet

1 teaspoon dried rosemary, divided
½ teaspoon garlic salt
½ teaspoon black pepper, divided
1 pound turkey breast cutlets, pounded to ¼-inch thickness
2 teaspoons canola oil, divided
1 can (about 15 ounces) no-salt-added navy beans or Great Northern beans, rinsed and drained
1 can (about 14 ounces) fire-roasted diced tomatoes
¼ cup grated Parmesan cheese

1. Combine ½ teaspoon rosemary, garlic salt and ¼ teaspoon pepper in small bowl; mix well. Sprinkle over turkey.

2. Heat 1 teaspoon oil in large nonstick skillet over medium heat. Add half of turkey; cook 2 to 3 minutes per side or until cooked through (165°F). Transfer to large platter; tent with foil to keep warm. Repeat with remaining 1 teaspoon oil and half of turkey.

3. Add beans, tomatoes, remaining ½ teaspoon rosemary and ¼ teaspoon pepper to same skillet. Bring to a boil over high heat. Reduce heat; simmer 5 minutes.

4. To serve, spoon bean mixture over and around turkey. Sprinkle with cheese. *Makes 6 servings*

Nutrients per Serving (⅙ of total recipe): Calories: 230, Total Fat: 4g, Saturated Fat: 1g, Cholesterol: 36mg, Sodium: 334mg, Carbohydrate: 23g, Fiber: 9g, Protein: 25g

chicken breasts with crabmeat stuffing

½ cup low-fat (1%) milk

¾ cup whole wheat cracker crumbs, divided

1 tablespoon dried parsley flakes

1 teaspoon paprika

1 teaspoon black pepper

3 ounces canned crabmeat, rinsed twice and drained

¼ cup fat-free mayonnaise

2 tablespoons grated Parmesan cheese

2 tablespoons finely chopped green onion

2 tablespoons lemon juice

¼ teaspoon hot pepper sauce

4 (4-ounce) boneless skinless chicken breasts, pounded to ¼-inch thickness

Microwave Directions

1. Place milk in shallow dish; set aside. Combine ½ cup cracker crumbs, parsley flakes, paprika and black pepper in another shallow dish; set aside.

2. Combine remaining ¼ cup cracker crumbs, crabmeat, mayonnaise, cheese, green onion, lemon juice and hot pepper sauce in medium bowl; mix well. Spoon evenly into center of chicken breasts. Roll up each chicken breast from short side, tucking in ends; secure with toothpick.

3. Dip chicken in milk; roll in cracker crumb mixture. Reserve remaining milk. Place chicken in microwavable dish. Cover with waxed paper. Microwave on HIGH 10 minutes or until chicken is cooked through (165°F). Remove chicken to serving plate.

4. Pour reserved milk into dish with pan juices; microwave on HIGH 1 minute. Spoon sauce evenly over chicken. *Makes 4 servings*

Nutrients per Serving (1 stuffed breast with ¼ of sauce): Calories: 246, Total Fat: 5g, Saturated Fat: 2g, Cholesterol: 83mg, Sodium: 424mg, Carbohydrate: 21g, Fiber: <1g, Protein: 30g

chicken breast with crabmeat stuffing

classic lasagna

6 whole wheat lasagna noodles
½ pound extra-lean ground beef
1 cup chopped onion
2 cloves garlic, minced
1 jar (26 ounces) tomato-basil pasta sauce
1 container (15 ounces) fat-free cottage cheese
2 egg whites
4 tablespoons chopped fresh basil, divided
2 cups (8 ounces) shredded part-skim mozzarella cheese, divided

1. Preheat oven to 375°F.

2. Cook noodles according to package directions, omitting salt and fat; drain. Rinse with cold water; drain again. Set aside.

3. Brown beef, onion and garlic 6 to 8 minutes in large saucepan over medium-high heat, stirring to break up meat. Drain fat. Add pasta sauce; bring to a boil. Reduce heat; simmer 5 minutes.

4. Stir cottage cheese, egg whites and 2 tablespoons basil in medium bowl until just combined. Spoon 1 cup sauce mixture over bottom of 13×9-inch baking dish. Layer three noodles over sauce mixture. Spoon cottage cheese mixture over noodles. Top with half of remaining sauce mixture and 1 cup mozzarella cheese. Top with remaining three noodles and pasta sauce mixture.

5. Cover with foil. Bake 30 minutes or until heated through.

6. Remove foil; sprinkle with remaining 1 cup mozzarella cheese and 2 tablespoons basil. Bake 5 minutes or until cheese is melted. Let stand 5 minutes before serving. *Makes 8 servings*

Nutrients per Serving (⅛ of total recipe): Calories: 252, Total Fat: 7g, Saturated Fat: 3g, Cholesterol: 35mg, Sodium: 676mg, Carbohydrate: 25g, Fiber: 5g, Protein: 25g

classic lasagna

thai-style pork kabobs

⅓ cup reduced-sodium soy sauce

2 tablespoons fresh lime juice

2 tablespoons water

2 teaspoons hot chili oil*

2 cloves garlic, minced

1 teaspoon minced fresh ginger

12 ounces well-trimmed pork tenderloin

1 red or yellow bell pepper, cut into ½-inch pieces

1 red or sweet onion, cut into ½-inch chunks

2 cups hot cooked rice

If hot chili oil is not available, combine 2 teaspoons vegetable oil and ½ teaspoon red pepper flakes in small microwavable bowl. Microwave on HIGH 30 to 45 seconds. Let stand 5 minutes to allow flavors to develop.

1. Whisk soy sauce, lime juice, water, chili oil, garlic and ginger in medium bowl until well blended. Reserve ⅓ cup for dipping sauce.

2. Cut pork tenderloin into ½-inch strips. Add to remaining soy sauce mixture; toss to coat evenly. Cover; refrigerate at least 30 minutes or up to 2 hours, turning once.

3. Spray grid with nonstick cooking spray. Prepare grill for direct cooking.

4. Remove pork from marinade; discard marinade. Alternately thread pork strips, bell pepper and onion onto eight 8- to 10-inch skewers.**

5. Grill, covered, over medium heat 6 to 8 minutes or until pork is barely pink in center, turning halfway through grilling time.

6. Serve with rice and reserved dipping sauce.   *Makes 4 servings*

**If using wooden skewers, soak in cold water 30 minutes to prevent burning.

Nutrients per Serving (2 kabobs with ½ cup rice and about 1 tablespoon plus 1 teaspoon dipping sauce): Calories: 248, Total Fat: 4g, Saturated Fat: 1g, Cholesterol: 49mg, Sodium: 271mg, Carbohydrate: 30g, Fiber: 2g, Protein: 22g

thai-style pork kabobs

sweet potato shepherd's pie

1 large sweet potato, peeled and cubed
1 large russet potato, peeled and cubed
¼ cup fat-free (skim) milk
¾ teaspoon salt
1 pound 93% lean ground turkey
2 packages (4 ounces each) sliced mixed mushrooms
    or 8 ounces sliced cremini mushrooms
1 jar (12 ounces) beef gravy
½ teaspoon dried thyme
¼ teaspoon black pepper
¾ cup frozen baby peas, thawed
   Nonstick cooking spray

1. Place sweet potato and russet potato in medium saucepan. Cover with water; bring to a boil over medium-high heat. Reduce heat; cover and simmer 20 minutes or until potatoes are very tender. Drain potatoes; return to saucepan. Mash potatoes with potato masher; stir in milk and salt.

2. Crumble turkey into large nonstick ovenproof skillet. Add mushrooms; cook and stir over medium-high heat until turkey is no longer pink and mushrooms begin to give off liquid. Drain.

3. Combine turkey mixture, gravy, thyme and pepper in same skillet; simmer 5 minutes. Add peas; cook and stir until heated through. Remove from heat. Spread potato mixture over turkey mixture; spray with cooking spray.

4. Preheat broiler. Broil 4 to 5 inches from heat source 5 minutes or until mixture is heated through and potatoes begin to brown.

Makes 6 servings

Nutrients per Serving (⅙ of total recipe): Calories: 188, Total Fat: 3g, Saturated Fat: 1g, Cholesterol: 32mg, Sodium: 689mg, Carbohydrate: 19g, Fiber: 3g, Protein: 23g

sweet potato shepherd's pie

bolognese sauce & penne pasta

8 ounces 95% lean ground beef
⅓ cup chopped onion
1 clove garlic, minced
1 can (8 ounces) tomato sauce
⅓ cup chopped carrot
¼ cup water
2 tablespoons red wine
1 teaspoon Italian seasoning
1½ cups hot cooked penne pasta
Chopped fresh parsley

1. Brown beef, onion and garlic 6 to 8 minutes in medium saucepan over medium-high heat, stirring to break up meat. Drain fat.

2. Add tomato sauce, carrot, water, wine and Italian seasoning; bring to a boil. Reduce heat; simmer 15 minutes.

3. Serve sauce over pasta. Sprinkle with parsley.   *Makes 2 servings*

Nutrients per Serving (½ of total recipe): Calories: 292, Total Fat: 5g, Saturated Fat: 2g, Cholesterol: 45mg, Sodium: 734mg, Carbohydrate: 40g, Fiber: 4g, Protein: 21g

bolognese sauce & penne pasta

sausage & shrimp jambalaya

1 teaspoon olive oil

1 cup chopped onion

1 large green bell pepper, cut into ¾-inch pieces

2 cloves garlic, minced

1¼ cups reduced-sodium chicken broth

1 can (about 14 ounces) diced tomatoes

⅔ cup uncooked rice

1 teaspoon dried thyme

½ teaspoon paprika

¼ teaspoon black pepper

8 ounces frozen medium cooked peeled shrimp

3 ounces kielbasa sausage, cut into ¼-inch slices

Hot pepper sauce (optional)

1. Heat oil in large nonstick skillet over medium heat. Add onion and bell pepper; cook and stir 4 to 5 minutes. Add garlic; cook and stir 30 seconds. Add broth, tomatoes, rice, thyme, paprika and black pepper; bring to a boil. Reduce heat to low; cover and simmer 15 minutes.

2. Stir in shrimp and sausage; cover and simmer 5 minutes or until shrimp are heated through and rice is tender. Sprinkle with hot pepper sauce, if desired. *Makes 5 servings*

Nutrients per Serving (1¼ cups): Calories: 210, Total Fat: 3g, Saturated Fat: <1g, Cholesterol: 102mg, Sodium: 553mg, Carbohydrate: 28g, Fiber: 2g, Protein: 17g

sausage & shrimp jambalaya

cashew chicken

10 ounces boneless skinless chicken breasts, cut into 1×½-inch pieces

1 tablespoon cornstarch

1 tablespoon dry white wine

1 tablespoon reduced-sodium soy sauce

½ teaspoon garlic powder

1 teaspoon vegetable oil

6 green onions, cut into 1-inch pieces

2 cups sliced fresh mushrooms

1 red or green bell pepper, cut into strips

1 can (6 ounces) sliced water chestnuts, rinsed and drained

2 tablespoons hoisin sauce (optional)

2 cups hot cooked white rice

¼ cup cashews, toasted*

To toast cashews, spread in single layer in heavy-bottomed skillet. Cook over medium heat 1 to 2 minutes, stirring frequently, until nuts are lightly browned. Remove from skillet immediately. Cool before using.

1. Place chicken in large resealable food storage bag. Whisk cornstarch, wine, soy sauce and garlic powder in small bowl until smooth and well blended. Pour over chicken. Seal bag; turn to coat evenly. Marinate in refrigerator 1 hour.

2. Drain chicken; discard marinade. Heat oil in wok or large nonstick skillet over medium-high heat. Add green onions; stir-fry 1 minute. Add chicken; stir-fry 2 minutes or until browned. Add mushrooms, bell pepper and water chestnuts; stir-fry 3 minutes or until vegetables are crisp-tender and chicken is cooked through. Stir in hoisin sauce, if desired; cook and stir 1 minute or until heated through.

3. Serve chicken and vegetables over rice. Top with cashews.

Makes 4 servings

Nutrients per Serving (1 cup stir-fry mixture with ½ cup rice and 1 tablespoon cashews): Calories: 274, Total Fat: 7g, Saturated Fat: 1g, Cholesterol: 36mg, Sodium: 83mg, Carbohydrate: 34g, Fiber: 3g, Protein: 18g

cashew chicken

artichoke, olive and goat cheese pizza

New York-Style Pizza Crust (recipe follows)
2 teaspoons olive oil
2 teaspoons minced fresh rosemary leaves *or* 1 teaspoon
    dried rosemary
3 cloves garlic, minced
½ cup (2 ounces) shredded Monterey Jack cheese
½ cup water-packed artichoke hearts, sliced
4 sun-dried tomatoes, packed in oil, drained and sliced
    (about ½ cup)
2½ ounces soft goat cheese, sliced or crumbled
10 kalamata olives, pitted and halved (about ¼ cup)

1. Prepare New York-Style Pizza Crust. Preheat oven to 500°F.

2. Brush olive oil over prepared crust. Sprinkle with rosemary and garlic; brush again to coat evenly with oil. Bake 3 to 4 minutes or until crust is light golden brown.

3. Sprinkle crust with half of Monterey Jack cheese, leaving 1-inch border. Top with artichokes, sun-dried tomatoes, goat cheese and olives. Sprinkle with remaining Monterey Jack cheese.

4. Bake 3 to 4 minutes or until crust is deep golden brown and cheese is melted. *Makes 4 servings*

Nutrients per Serving (¼ of total recipe): Calories: 262, Total Fat: 14g, Saturated Fat: 6g, Cholesterol: 23mg, Sodium: 505mg, Carbohydrate: 26g, Fiber: 2g, Protein: 10g

new york-style pizza crust

⅓ cup warm water (110° to 115°F)
½ teaspoon sugar
½ teaspoon active dry yeast
¾ cup plus 2 tablespoons all-purpose or bread flour, divided
¼ teaspoon salt

1. Combine water and sugar in small bowl; stir to dissolve sugar. Sprinkle yeast over water; stir. Let stand 5 to 10 minutes or until foamy.

2. Combine ¾ cup flour and salt in medium bowl. Stir in yeast mixture until soft dough forms.

continued on page 84

artichoke, olive and goat cheese pizza

new york-style pizza crust, continued

3. Place dough on lightly floured surface. Knead 5 minutes or until dough is smooth and elastic, adding remaining flour, 1 tablespoon at a time, if necessary.

4. Place dough in large bowl coated with nonstick cooking spray. Turn dough to coat evenly with cooking spray; cover with towel or plastic wrap. Let rise in warm place 30 minutes or until doubled in size.

5. Punch dough down; place on lightly floured surface and knead 2 minutes or until smooth. Pat dough into flat disc. Let rest 2 to 3 minutes.

6. Pat and gently stretch dough into 10- to 11-inch circle, allowing it to rest for a few minutes if it becomes hard to stretch. Transfer to baking sheet sprayed with cooking spray or pizza peel. Proceed as recipe directs.   *Makes 1 (10- to 11-inch) pizza crust*

roasted rosemary chicken legs

263
calories

¼ **cup finely chopped onion**

2 **tablespoons margarine or butter, melted**

1 **tablespoon chopped fresh rosemary leaves** *or* 1 **teaspoon dried rosemary**

½ **teaspoon salt**

¼ **teaspoon black pepper**

2 **cloves garlic, minced**

4 **chicken legs (about 1½ pounds)**

¼ **cup white wine or chicken broth**

1. Preheat oven to 375°F.

2. Combine onion, margarine, rosemary, salt, pepper and garlic in small bowl; mix well. Gently loosen chicken skin; rub onion mixture under and over skin. Place chicken, skin side up, in small shallow roasting pan. Pour wine over chicken.

3. Roast chicken 50 to 60 minutes or until chicken is browned and cooked through (165°F), basting frequently with pan juices.   *Makes 4 servings*

Nutrients per Serving (¼ of total recipe): Calories: 263, Total Fat: 17g, Saturated Fat: 5g, Cholesterol: 77mg, Sodium: 407mg, Carbohydrate: 2g, Fiber: <1g, Protein: 22g

honey glazed pork

1¼ **pounds pork tenderloin (about 1 large or 2 small)**

¼ **cup reduced-sodium soy sauce**

2 **cloves garlic, minced**

3 **tablespoons honey**

2 **tablespoons packed brown sugar**

1 **teaspoon minced fresh ginger**

1 **tablespoon sesame seeds, toasted***

*To toast sesame seeds, spread in small skillet. Shake skillet over medium heat 2 minutes or until seeds begin to pop and turn golden.

1. Place pork in large resealable food storage bag. Whisk soy sauce and garlic in small bowl until well blended. Pour over pork. Seal bag; turn to coat evenly. Marinate in refrigerator up to 2 hours.

2. Preheat oven to 400°F. Line shallow roasting pan with foil.

3. Drain pork; reserve 1 tablespoon marinade. Whisk honey, brown sugar, ginger and reserved marinade in small bowl until smooth and well blended.

4. Place pork in prepared roasting pan. Brush with half of honey mixture. Roast 10 minutes.

5. Turn pork; brush with remaining honey mixture. Sprinkle with sesame seeds. Roast 10 to 15 minutes or until cooked through (155°F).

6. Tent pork with foil; let stand 5 minutes before slicing. (Temperature of pork will rise to 160°F.)   *Makes 4 servings*

Nutrients per Serving (¼ of total recipe): Calories: 279, Total Fat: 6g, Saturated Fat: 2g, Cholesterol: 101mg, Sodium: 605mg, Carbohydrate: 21g, Fiber: <1g, Protein: 33g

enlightened tuna noodle casserole

4 ounces uncooked elbow macaroni

1 tablespoon olive oil

¾ cup chopped onion

½ cup thinly sliced celery

½ cup chopped red bell pepper

2 tablespoons whole wheat flour

1 teaspoon dried thyme

⅛ teaspoon white pepper

1½ cups fat-free reduced-sodium vegetable broth, warmed

2 pouches (3 ounces each) albacore tuna

½ cup fat-free cottage cheese

1 teaspoon ground paprika

Fresh dill sprigs (optional)

1. Preheat oven to 375°F. Spray 8-inch square baking dish with nonstick cooking spray.

2. Cook macaroni according to package directions, omitting salt and fat. Drain; set aside.

3. Heat oil in large nonstick skillet over medium heat. Add onion; cook and stir 3 minutes. Add celery and bell pepper; cook and stir 3 minutes. Sprinkle flour, thyme and white pepper over vegetables; cook and stir 1 minute. Gradually stir in broth; cook and stir until thickened. Remove from heat.

4. Stir macaroni, tuna and cottage cheese into skillet until well combined and macaroni is evenly coated. Transfer to prepared dish; sprinkle with paprika.

5. Bake 20 to 25 minutes or until heated through. Garnish with dill sprigs.

Makes 4 servings

Nutrients per Serving (¼ of total recipe): Calories: 231, Total Fat: 4g, Saturated Fat: <1g, Cholesterol: 10mg, Sodium: 369mg, Carbohydrate: 30g, Fiber: 3g, Protein: 15g

enlightened tuna noodle casserole

beef & artichoke casserole

¾ **pound 95% lean ground beef**

½ **cup sliced mushrooms**

¼ **cup chopped onion**

 1 **clove garlic, minced**

 1 **can (14 ounces) artichoke hearts, drained and chopped**

½ **cup dry bread crumbs**

¼ **cup (1 ounce) grated Parmesan cheese**

 1 **tablespoon chopped fresh rosemary leaves** *or* **1 teaspoon dried rosemary**

1½ **teaspoons chopped fresh marjoram** *or* **½ teaspoon dried marjoram**
   Salt and black pepper

 3 **egg whites**

1. Preheat oven to 400°F. Spray 1-quart casserole with nonstick cooking spray.

2. Brown beef 6 to 8 minutes in medium skillet over medium-high heat, stirring to break up meat. Drain fat. Add mushrooms, onion and garlic; cook and stir 5 minutes or until tender.

3. Combine ground beef mixture, artichokes, bread crumbs, cheese, rosemary and marjoram; gently mix. Season with salt and pepper.

4. Beat egg whites in medium bowl with electric mixer at high speed until stiff peaks form; fold into ground beef mixture. Spoon into prepared casserole.

5. Bake 20 minutes or until edges are lightly browned.

Makes 4 servings

Nutrients per Serving (¼ of total recipe): Calories: 260, Total Fat: 7g, Saturated Fat: 3g, Cholesterol: 55mg, Sodium: 330mg, Carbohydrate: 24g, Fiber: 9g, Protein: 28g

beef & artichoke casserole

salmon with dill-mustard sauce

2 tablespoons fresh lemon juice

2 tablespoons fresh lime juice

4 salmon fillets (4 ounces each)

¼ cup fat-free mayonnaise

1 tablespoon Dijon mustard

1 tablespoon chopped fresh dill sprigs, plus additional for garnish

1. Combine lemon juice and lime juice in glass baking dish. Rinse salmon; pat dry. Place salmon in baking dish; turn to coat evenly. Marinate 10 minutes, turning once.

2. Stir mayonnaise, mustard and 1 tablespoon dill in small bowl until well blended.

3. Preheat broiler. Spray rack of broiler pan with nonstick cooking spray. Remove salmon from marinade; pat dry. Place on rack.

4. Broil 4 inches from heat source 3 to 4 minutes per side or until salmon begins to flake when tested with fork.

5. Place salmon on serving plates. Spoon evenly with sauce. Garnish with additional dill. *Makes 4 servings*

Nutrients per Serving (1 salmon fillet with about 1 tablespoon sauce):
Calories: 220, Total Fat: 12g, Saturated Fat: 3g, Cholesterol: 74mg,
Sodium: 260mg, Carbohydrate: 3g, Fiber: <1g, Protein: 23g

salmon with dill-mustard sauce

chunky black bean
and sweet potato chili

2 teaspoons vegetable oil

1 cup chopped sweet onion

2 red or green bell peppers or one of each, cut into ½-inch chunks

4 cloves garlic, minced

1 teaspoon chili powder

1 can (about 14 ounces) fire-roasted diced tomatoes

1 small sweet potato (8 ounces), peeled and cut into ½-inch chunks

1 tablespoon minced chipotle chile pepper in adobo sauce

1 can (about 15 ounces) black beans, rinsed and drained

½ cup chopped cilantro (optional)

1. Heat oil in large saucepan over medium heat. Add onion; cook and stir 5 minutes. Add bell peppers, garlic and chili powder; cook and stir 2 minutes. Add tomatoes, sweet potato and chipotle chile pepper; bring to a boil. Reduce heat to medium-low; cover and simmer 15 minutes.

2. Stir in black beans; cover and simmer 8 to 10 minutes or until vegetables are tender. (Chili will be thick; thin with water as desired.)

3. Ladle chili into five serving bowls; top with cilantro, if desired.

Makes 5 servings

Nutrients per Serving (1¼ cups): Calories: 156, Total Fat: 2g, Saturated Fat: 0g, Cholesterol: 0mg, Sodium: 546mg, Carbohydrate: 31g, Fiber: 8g, Protein: 6g

Note: Sweet potatoes do not need to be peeled but should be scrubbed under cold running water before cooking. Cooking with skins intact retains more nutrients. Sweet potatoes may be peeled first if they are going to be added raw to stews or soups.

chunky black bean and sweet potato chili

tilapia with spinach and feta

1 teaspoon olive oil

1 clove garlic, minced

4 cups baby spinach

2 skinless tilapia fillets or other mild whitefish (4 ounces each)

¼ teaspoon black pepper

2 ounces reduced-fat feta cheese, cut into 2 (3-inch) pieces

1. Preheat oven to 350°F. Spray baking sheet with nonstick cooking spray.

2. Heat oil in medium skillet over medium-low heat. Add garlic; cook and stir 2 minutes. Add spinach; cook just until wilted, stirring occasionally.

3. Arrange tilapia on prepared baking sheet; sprinkle with pepper. Place one piece of cheese on each fillet; top with spinach mixture.

4. Fold one end of each fillet up and over filling; secure with toothpick. Repeat with opposite end of each fillet.

5. Bake 20 minutes or until fish begins to flake when tested with fork.

Makes 2 servings

Nutrients per Serving (½ of total recipe): Calories: 193, Total Fat: 9g, Saturated Fat: 3g, Cholesterol: 10mg, Sodium: 531mg, Carbohydrate: 3g, Fiber: <1g, Protein: 26g

tilapia with spinach and feta

pastitsio

8 ounces uncooked elbow macaroni
½ cup cholesterol-free egg substitute
¼ teaspoon ground nutmeg
¾ pound lean ground lamb, beef or turkey
½ cup chopped onion
1 clove garlic, minced
1 can (8 ounces) tomato sauce
¾ teaspoon dried mint
½ teaspoon dried oregano
½ teaspoon black pepper
⅛ teaspoon ground cinnamon
2 teaspoons reduced-fat margarine
3 tablespoons all-purpose flour
1½ cups fat-free (skim) milk
2 tablespoons grated Parmesan cheese

1. Preheat oven to 350°F. Spray 9-inch square baking dish with nonstick cooking spray. Cook macaroni according to package directions, omitting salt and fat. Drain.

2. Combine macaroni, egg substitute and nutmeg in prepared baking dish; mix well.

3. Brown lamb, onion and garlic 6 to 8 minutes in large nonstick skillet over medium heat, stirring to break up meat. Drain. Stir in tomato sauce, mint, oregano, pepper and cinnamon. Reduce heat; simmer 10 minutes. Spread evenly over macaroni in baking dish.

4. Melt margarine in small saucepan. Add flour; cook and stir 1 minute. Whisk in milk; cook 6 minutes or until thickened, stirring constantly. Pour sauce over meat mixture. Sprinkle with cheese.

5. Bake 30 to 40 minutes. *Makes 6 servings*

Nutrients per Serving (⅙ of total recipe): Calories: 280, Total Fat: 5g, Saturated Fat: 2g, Cholesterol: 31mg, Sodium: 366mg, Carbohydrate: 39g, Fiber: 1g, Protein: 20g

pastitsio

chicken goulash

1 small onion, chopped

1 stalk celery, chopped

1 medium carrot, chopped

1 clove garlic, minced

½ cup reduced-sodium chicken broth

½ cup no-salt-added tomato purée

1 teaspoon paprika

¼ teaspoon dried marjoram or oregano

⅛ teaspoon black pepper

5 ounces boneless skinless chicken thighs, trimmed

1 small unpeeled new potato, diced

1 heaping teaspoon all-purpose flour

¼ teaspoon salt (optional)

Slow Cooker Directions

1. Combine onion, celery, carrot and garlic in slow cooker. Whisk broth, tomato purée, paprika, marjoram and pepper in small bowl until well blended; pour over vegetables. Add chicken and potato. Cover; cook on LOW 5 to 6 hours.

2. Whisk flour into 2 tablespoons cooking liquid from slow cooker in small bowl. Stir flour mixture into slow cooker. Cover; cook 10 minutes. Stir in salt, if desired. *Makes 2 servings*

Nutrients per Serving (1¼ cups): Calories: 226, Total Fat: 3g, Saturated Fat: <1g, Cholesterol: 60mg, Sodium: 156mg, Carbohydrate: 31g, Fiber: 5g, Protein: 19g

chicken goulash

Sandwiches & More

mediterranean vegetable sandwiches

- 1 small eggplant, peeled, halved and cut into ¼-inch-thick slices
  Salt
- 1 small zucchini, halved and cut lengthwise into ¼-inch-thick slices
- 1 red bell pepper, sliced
- 3 tablespoons balsamic vinegar
- ½ teaspoon garlic powder
- 2 French bread rolls, cut in half lengthwise

1. Place eggplant in non-aluminum colander; lightly sprinkle with salt. Let stand 30 minutes. Rinse eggplant; pat dry with paper towels.

2. Preheat broiler. Spray rack with nonstick cooking spray. Place vegetables on rack. Broil 4 inches from heat source 8 to 10 minutes or until vegetables are browned, turning once.

3. Whisk vinegar and garlic powder in medium bowl until well blended. Add vegetables; toss to coat evenly. Divide vegetable mixture evenly between rolls. Serve immediately. *Makes 2 sandwiches*

Nutrients per Serving (1 sandwich): Calories: 178, Total Fat: 2g, Saturated Fat: <1g, Cholesterol: 0mg, Sodium: 775mg, Carbohydrate: 36g, Fiber: 1g, Protein: 5g

170
calories

black bean and bell pepper burritos

2 teaspoons canola oil

1½ cups diced red, yellow and green bell peppers

½ cup chopped onion

1 can (about 15 ounces) black beans, rinsed and drained

½ cup salsa

1 teaspoon chili powder

7 (8-inch) whole wheat or multigrain low-carb flour tortillas, warmed

¾ cup (3 ounces) reduced-fat shredded Cheddar or Mexican cheese blend

½ cup chopped fresh cilantro

1. Heat oil in large nonstick skillet over medium heat. Add bell peppers and onion; cook and stir 3 to 4 minutes. Stir in beans, salsa and chili powder; cook and stir 5 to 8 minutes or until vegetables are tender and sauce is thickened.

2. Spoon about ⅔ cup bean mixture down center of each tortilla. Top with cheese and cilantro. Roll up to enclose filling.   *Makes 7 burritos*

Nutrients per Serving (1 burrito): Calories: 170, Total Fat: 4g, Saturated Fat: 1g, Cholesterol: 5mg, Sodium: 550mg, Carbohydrate: 31g, Fiber: 6g, Protein: 10g

black bean and bell pepper burrito

italian meatball subs

Nonstick cooking spray
½ cup chopped onion
3 teaspoons finely chopped garlic, divided
1 can (about 14 ounces) Italian-style crushed tomatoes, undrained
2 bay leaves
2½ teaspoons dried basil, divided
2 teaspoons dried oregano, divided
¾ teaspoon black pepper, divided
¼ teaspoon red pepper flakes
½ pound 95% lean ground beef
⅓ cup chopped green onions
⅓ cup plain dry bread crumbs
¼ cup chopped fresh parsley
1 egg white
2 tablespoons water
½ teaspoon dried marjoram
½ teaspoon ground mustard
4 French bread rolls, warmed and cut in half lengthwise

1. Spray large saucepan with cooking spray; heat over medium heat. Add onion and 2 teaspoons garlic; cook and stir 5 minutes or until onion is tender. Add tomatoes, bay leaves, 2 teaspoons basil, 1 teaspoon oregano, ½ teaspoon black pepper and red pepper flakes; cover and simmer 30 minutes, stirring occasionally.

2. Combine beef, green onions, bread crumbs, parsley, egg white, water, remaining 1 teaspoon garlic, ½ teaspoon basil, 1 teaspoon oregano, ¼ teaspoon black pepper, marjoram and mustard in medium bowl; mix well. Shape into 16 meatballs.

3. Spray large nonstick skillet with cooking spray; heat over medium heat. Add meatballs; cook 5 minutes or until meatballs are cooked through (160°F), turning occasionally.

4. Remove and discard bay leaves from tomato sauce. Add meatballs; cook 5 minutes, stirring occasionally.

5. Place 4 meatballs in each roll. Spoon additional sauce over meatballs. Serve immediately. *Makes 4 servings*

Nutrients per Serving (1 sub): Calories: 282, Total Fat: 9g, Saturated Fat: 3g, Cholesterol: 35mg, Sodium: 497mg, Carbohydrate: 32g, Fiber: 1g, Protein: 18g

italian meatball subs

turkey sliders

- **1 pound extra-lean ground turkey**
- **¼ cup finely chopped green onions**
- **2 tablespoons low-fat mayonnaise**
- **1 tablespoon Worcestershire sauce**
- **¼ teaspoon black pepper**
- **⅛ teaspoon salt**
- **12 baby spinach leaves**
- **¼ cup (1 ounce) shredded reduced-fat sharp Cheddar cheese**
- **1 shallot, thinly cut into 12 slices**
- **1 tablespoon steak sauce (optional)**
- **12 mini whole wheat pita bread rounds, cut in half horizontally**

1. Combine turkey, green onions, mayonnaise, Worcestershire sauce, black pepper and salt in large bowl; mix well. Shape into 12 patties.

2. Spray large nonstick skillet with nonstick cooking spray; heat over medium heat. Add patties; cook 5 minutes per side or until cooked through.

3. Layer spinach, patties, cheese, shallot and steak sauce, if desired, evenly on pita bottoms. Cover with pita tops.   *Makes 12 sliders*

Nutrients per Serving (2 sliders): Calories: 262, Total Fat: 4g, Saturated Fat: 1g, Cholesterol: 43mg, Sodium: 596mg, Carbohydrate: 31g, Fiber: 2g, Protein: 24g

Note: There are different varieties of ground turkey available. Regular ground turkey (85% lean) is a combination of white and dark meat, which is comparable in fat to some lean cuts of ground beef. Ground turkey breast is lowest in fat (up to 99% lean), but it can dry out very easily when grilled. To keep the best texture, gently form patties or meatballs and do not press down on the patties as they grill.

turkey sliders

mushroom, ham and cheese sandwiches

2 cups sliced mushrooms (about 4 ounces)
Pinch salt (optional)
Pinch black pepper
Pinch crushed dried rosemary
2 tablespoons low-fat mayonnaise
4 slices whole wheat bread, toasted
2 slices 96% fat-free, reduced-sodium ham
2 thin slices reduced-fat Swiss cheese

1. Spray large nonstick skillet with cooking spray; heat over medium-high heat. Add mushrooms; cook and stir 5 minutes or until lightly browned. Sprinkle with salt, if desired, pepper and rosemary.

2. Spread mayonnaise on half of bread slices. Top evenly with mushrooms, ham, cheese and remaining bread slices.   *Makes 2 sandwiches*

Nutrients per Serving (1 sandwich): Calories: 263, Total Fat: 8g, Saturated Fat: 3g, Cholesterol: 20mg, Sodium: 619mg, Carbohydrate: 32g, Fiber: 3g, Protein: 19g

mushroom, ham and cheese sandwich

grilled chipotle chicken sandwiches

½ cup fat-free sour cream

2 tablespoons light mayonnaise

1 canned chipotle pepper in adobo sauce

2 teaspoons adobo sauce from canned chipotle

⅛ teaspoon salt (optional)

1 medium lime, divided

4 boneless skinless chicken breasts (4 ounces each), flattened slightly
   Black pepper

2 slices Swiss cheese, cut in half diagonally

4 whole wheat hamburger buns, split

4 leaves romaine lettuce

4 thin slices red onion

1. Spray grid with nonstick cooking spray. Prepare grill for direct cooking.

2. Combine sour cream, mayonnaise, chipotle pepper, adobo sauce and salt, if desired, in food processor or blender; process until smooth.

3. Squeeze juice from half of lime evenly over chicken. Grill chicken over medium-high heat 10 minutes.

4. Turn chicken over; sprinkle with black pepper. Grill 10 minutes or until chicken is cooked through (165°F).

5. Move chicken to side of grill. Squeeze remaining lime half over chicken; top with cheese. Meanwhile, place cut sides of buns on grill; toast lightly.

6. Arrange lettuce, chicken and onion evenly on bun bottoms. Spread toasted bun tops with chipotle mixture; add to sandwich.

Makes 4 sandwiches

Nutrients per Serving (1 sandwich): Calories: 299, Total Fat: 8g, Saturated Fat: 3g, Cholesterol: 82mg, Sodium: 798mg, Carbohydrate: 22g, Fiber: 3g, Protein: 33g

grilled chipotle chicken sandwich

deli beef wraps with creamy honey mustard spread

3 tablespoons light mayonnaise

1 tablespoon honey mustard

1½ teaspoons packed dark brown sugar (optional)

4 whole grain or whole wheat tortillas

2 cups packed shredded lettuce

6 ounces thinly sliced deli roast beef

1 medium green bell pepper, thinly sliced

¼ cup thinly sliced red onion

1. Stir mayonnaise, honey mustard and brown sugar, if desired, in small bowl until well blended. Spread evenly on tortillas.

2. Layer lettuce, roast beef, bell pepper and onion evenly on tortillas. Roll up to enclose filling. Serve immediately or refrigerate up to 6 hours.

Makes 4 wraps

Nutrients per Serving (1 wrap): Calories: 245, Total Fat: 10g, Saturated Fat: 2g, Cholesterol: 24mg, Sodium: 825mg, Carbohydrate: 28g, Fiber: 2g, Protein: 11g

Variation: Stir chopped fresh cilantro into the mayonnaise mixture and add a layer of chopped avocado.

deli beef wrap with creamy honey mustard spread

southwestern sloppy joes

1 pound lean ground beef

1 cup chopped onion

¼ cup chopped celery

¼ cup water

1 can (10 ounces) diced tomatoes and green chiles

1 can (8 ounces) no-salt-added tomato sauce

4 teaspoons packed brown sugar

½ teaspoon ground cumin

¼ teaspoon salt

9 whole wheat hamburger buns

1. Brown beef, onion, celery and water 6 to 8 minutes in large nonstick skillet over medium heat, stirring to break up meat.

2. Stir in tomatoes, tomato sauce, brown sugar, cumin and salt; bring to a boil over high heat. Reduce heat; simmer 20 minutes or until mixture is thickened. Serve on buns.   *Makes 9 servings*

Nutrients per Serving (1 sloppy joe): Calories: 190, Total Fat: 4g, Saturated Fat: 1g, Cholesterol: 15mg, Sodium: 413mg, Carbohydrate: 26g, Fiber: 1g, Protein: 13g

southwestern sloppy joe

hoisin barbecue chicken sliders

⅔ **cup hoisin sauce**

⅓ **cup barbecue sauce**

3 **tablespoons quick-cooking tapioca**

1 **tablespoon sugar**

1 **tablespoon reduced-sodium soy sauce**

¼ **teaspoon red pepper flakes**

12 **boneless, skinless chicken thighs (3 to 3½ pounds total)**

16 **dinner rolls or Hawaiian sweet rolls, split**

½ **medium red onion, finely chopped**

Sliced pickles (optional)

Slow Cooker Directions

1. Combine hoisin sauce, barbecue sauce, tapioca, sugar, soy sauce and red pepper flakes in slow cooker; mix well. Add chicken. Cover; cook on LOW 8 to 9 hours.

2. Remove chicken from sauce. Coarsely shred with two forks. Return shredded chicken and any sauce to slow cooker; mix well.

3. Spoon ¼ cup chicken and sauce on each bun. Top each with about 1 teaspoon chopped red onion and pickles, if desired.

Makes 16 sliders

Nutrients per Serving (1 slider): Calories: 280, Total Fat: 8g, Saturated Fat: 3g, Cholesterol: 75mg, Sodium: 500mg, Carbohydrate: 35g, Fiber: 13g, Protein: 22g

hoisin barbecue chicken sliders

black bean burgers

2 cans (about 15 ounces each) black beans, rinsed
and drained, divided
¾ cup plain dry bread crumbs
⅔ cup finely chopped green onions
2 egg whites
¼ cup chopped fresh basil
2 teaspoons onion powder
2 teaspoons dried oregano
1 teaspoon baking powder
1 teaspoon ground cumin
1 teaspoon black pepper
½ teaspoon salt
¾ cup corn
¾ cup chopped roasted red pepper
Nonstick cooking spray
6 whole wheat hamburger buns
Avocado slices (optional)
Salsa (optional)

1. Combine half of beans, bread crumbs, green onions, egg whites, basil, onion powder, oregano, baking powder, cumin, black pepper and salt in food processor; process using on/off pulsing action 30 to 40 seconds or until mixture begins to hold together. Stir in remaining beans, corn and roasted red pepper. Let stand 20 minutes to allow flavors to develop.

2. Preheat oven to 350°F. Line baking sheet with parchment paper.

3. Shape mixture into six patties. Place on prepared baking sheet; spray with cooking spray.

4. Bake 18 to 20 minutes or until patties are firm.

5. Serve on buns; top with avocado and salsa, if desired.

Makes 6 burgers

Nutrients per Serving (1 burger): Calories: 149, Total Fat: 2g, Saturated Fat: <1g, Cholesterol: 0mg, Sodium: 696mg, Carbohydrate: 31g, Fiber: 6g, Protein: 7g

Tip: Cooked burgers can be wrapped up and frozen to save for grilling season. Just grill burgers over medium-high heat until heated through.

black bean burger

chicken and grape pita sandwiches

1 quart water

1 pound boneless skinless chicken breasts, cut into ½-inch pieces

½ cup plain nonfat yogurt

¼ cup reduced-fat mayonnaise

2 tablespoons fresh tarragon leaves, minced, *or* 2 teaspoons dried tarragon

2 teaspoons Dijon mustard

2 teaspoons honey

½ teaspoon black pepper

1 cup thinly sliced celery

1 cup red seedless grapes, cut into halves

1 medium head red leaf lettuce

3 white pita bread rounds, cut in half crosswise

1. Bring water to a boil in large saucepan. Add chicken; cover and remove from heat. Let stand 6 minutes or until chicken is cooked through (165°F). Drain. Rinse chicken under cold water; drain.

2. Stir yogurt, mayonnaise, tarragon, mustard, honey and pepper in large bowl until well blended. Add chicken, celery and grapes; toss to coat evenly. Separate lettuce leaves. Select six large leaves and discard stems. Tear or shred remaining leaves.

3. Line each pita half with whole lettuce leaf. Fill with handful of torn lettuce leaves and about ⅔ cup chicken mixture.

Makes 6 sandwiches

Nutrients per Serving (1 pita half): Calories: 249, Total Fat: 6g, Saturated Fat: 1g, Cholesterol: 50mg, Sodium: 278mg, Carbohydrate: 28g, Fiber: 1g, Protein: 22g

chicken and grape pita sandwich

open-faced reubens

1 cup shredded cabbage

2 tablespoons reduced-fat mayonnaise, divided

2 tablespoons reduced-sodium or no-salt-added chili sauce, divided

4 slices pumpernickel or rye bread, toasted

4 ounces sliced pastrami

2 slices reduced-fat Swiss cheese, cut into ½-inch strips

1. Preheat broiler. Combine cabbage, 1 tablespoon mayonnaise and 1 tablespoon chili sauce in medium bowl; mix well.

2. Stir remaining 1 tablespoon mayonnaise and 1 tablespoon chili sauce in small bowl until well blended. Spread mayonnaise mixture over half of bread slices. Top each with 1 ounce pastrami, ¼ cup cabbage mixture and one fourth of cheese strips. Place on baking sheet.

3. Broil 4 to 5 inches from heat source 40 seconds to 1 minute or until cheese is melted.   *Makes 4 servings*

Nutrients per Serving (1 reuben): Calories: 164, Total Fat: 4g, Saturated Fat: 2g, Cholesterol: 24mg, Sodium: 670mg, Carbohydrate: 21g, Fiber: 3g, Protein: 12g

Tip: To reduce the sodium in this recipe, make the sauce by combining 2 tablespoons low-fat mayonnaise, 1 tablespoon no-salt-added chili sauce and $\frac{1}{16}$ teaspoon red pepper flakes.

Note: Cabbage is a cruciferous vegetable and in the same family as kale, Brussels sprouts, broccoli and collard greens. It's an excellent source of vitamin C and a very good source of fiber, folic acid and omega-3 fatty acids.

open-faced reuben

asian cilantro wraps

Sauce

> **2 tablespoons raspberry or strawberry fruit spread**
>
> **2 tablespoons reduced-sodium soy sauce**
>
> **⅛ teaspoon red pepper flakes**

Filling

> **2 teaspoons canola oil**
>
> **3 cups thinly sliced purple cabbage**
>
> **6 ounces asparagus spears, trimmed and cut into ½-inch
> pieces (about 1½ cups)**
>
> **½ cup thinly sliced carrots**
>
> **1 cup chopped green onions**
>
> **4 (6-inch) low-carb flour tortillas, warmed**
>
> **¼ cup chopped cilantro**
>
> **¼ cup peanuts, chopped**
>
> **1 cup diced cooked chicken breast**

1. Microwave fruit spread in small microwavable bowl on HIGH
15 seconds or until slightly melted. Stir in soy sauce and red pepper
flakes; set aside.

2. Heat oil in large nonstick skillet over medium-high heat. Add cabbage,
asparagus and carrots; cook and stir 2 minutes. Add green onions; cook
and stir 2 to 3 minutes or until cabbage is slightly wilted. Remove from
heat.

3. Spoon about 1 cup filling on each tortilla. Top each with 1 tablespoon
sauce, 1 tablespoon cilantro, 1 tablespoon peanuts and ¼ cup chicken.
Roll up to enclose filling.   *Makes 4 wraps*

Nutrients per Serving (1 wrap): Calories: 227, Total Fat: 9g, Saturated Fat: 1g,
Cholesterol: 27mg, Sodium: 510mg, Carbohydrate: 27g, Fiber: 11g, Protein: 21g

asian cilantro wrap

lean beef burgers

1 pound extra-lean ground beef
¼ cup finely chopped sweet or yellow onion
1 teaspoon garlic salt
  Black pepper (optional)
2 tablespoons low-fat mayonnaise
1 tablespoon ketchup
4 red leaf or Boston lettuce leaves
4 multigrain sandwich thins
4 slices large tomato

1. Spray grid with cooking spray. Prepare grill for direct cooking.

2. Combine beef, onion and garlic salt; mix well. Shape into four patties. Sprinkle with pepper, if desired.

3. Grill over medium heat 4 to 5 minutes per side or until cooked through (160°F).

4. Stir mayonnaise and ketchup in small bowl until well blended. Layer lettuce over bottoms of sandwich thins; top evenly with patties, mayonnaise mixture and tomato. Cover with sandwich thin tops.

Makes 4 burgers

Nutrients per Serving (1 burger): Calories: 272, Total Fat: 7g, Saturated Fat: 2g, Cholesterol: 70mg, Sodium: 617mg, Carbohydrate: 25g, Fiber: 6g, Protein: 30g

lean beef burger

curried tuna salad on raisin toast

**2 cans (6 ounces each) tuna packed in water, rinsed and
   well drained**

3 tablespoons light mayonnaise

**2 tablespoons fat-free sour cream or plain nonfat yogurt
   or 1 tablespoon fat-free (skim) milk**

1 to 1½ tablespoons sugar

1 teaspoon curry powder

¼ teaspoon ground cumin

**½ (8-ounce can) sliced water chestnuts, drained and coarsely
   chopped**

⅛ teaspoon ground red pepper

**4 slices cinnamon-raisin bread, lightly toasted and cut
   in half diagonally**

1. Combine tuna, mayonnaise, sour cream, sugar, curry powder and cumin in medium bowl; mix well. Add water chestnuts and red pepper; mix well. Cover and refrigerate 15 minutes to allow flavors to develop.

2. Arrange toast halves on serving plates. Spoon tuna mixture evenly onto toast halves.   *Makes 4 servings*

Nutrients per Serving (2 toast halves with about ½ cup tuna salad):
Calories: 233, Total Fat: 5g, Saturated Fat: <1g, Cholesterol: 31mg,
Sodium: 465mg, Carbohydrate: 22g, Fiber: 2g, Protein: 24g

curried tuna salad on raisin toast

Side
Dishes

rice pilaf with dried cherries and almonds

½ **cup slivered almonds**
2 **tablespoons butter**
2 **cups converted white rice**
½ **cup chopped onion**
1 **can (about 14 ounces) vegetable broth**
1½ **cups water**
½ **cup dried cherries**

1. Heat large nonstick skillet over medium heat. Add almonds; cook and stir 1 to 2 minutes or until lightly browned. Remove from skillet; cool completely.

2. Melt butter in same skillet over low heat. Add rice and onion; cook and stir until rice is lightly browned. Add broth and water; bring to a boil over high heat. Reduce heat to low; cover and simmer 15 minutes.

3. Stir in almonds and cherries. Simmer 5 minutes or until liquid is absorbed and rice is tender. *Makes 12 servings*

Nutrients per Serving (½ cup): Calories: 174, Total Fat: 5g, Saturated Fat: 1g, Cholesterol: 0mg, Sodium: 37mg, Carbohydrate: 29g, Fiber: 1g, Protein: 3g

quick mashed potatoes with cauliflower

16 ounces russet potatoes, peeled and cut into 2-inch chunks
1 small cauliflower, trimmed into florets (about 4 to 5 cups)
¼ cup water
2 tablespoons vegetable oil spread
2 cloves garlic, minced
½ teaspoon salt
¼ teaspoon black pepper
2 tablespoons chopped chives

1. Place potatoes in medium saucepan; cover with water. Cover; bring to a boil. Reduce heat; simmer 15 minutes or until tender. Drain.

2. Meanwhile, place cauliflower and ¼ cup water in microwavable dish. Cover; microwave on HIGH 5 minutes or until just tender. Drain.

3. Combine potatoes and cauliflower in large bowl. Mash with potato masher. Add vegetable oil spread, garlic, salt and pepper; mix well. Sprinkle with chives. *Makes 4 servings*

Nutrients per Serving (about ¾ cup): Calories: 168, Total Fat: 5g, Saturated Fat: 1g, Cholesterol: 0mg, Sodium: 364mg, Carbohydrate: 28g, Fiber: 4g, Protein: 4g

Note: Adding mashed cauliflower to mashed potatoes cuts down on the total number of calories and carbohydrates.

Tip: If you like the texture of the potatoes mashed with a potato masher, but you don't like the graininess of the cauliflower mashed this way, use a hand mixer for the cauliflower before adding the drained potatoes. Then mash with the potato masher.

quick mashed potatoes with cauliflower

confetti black beans

1 cup dried black beans

3 cups water

1 can (about 14 ounces) reduced-sodium chicken broth

1 bay leaf

1½ teaspoons olive oil

1 medium onion, chopped

¼ cup chopped red bell pepper

¼ cup chopped yellow bell pepper

2 cloves garlic, minced

1 jalapeño pepper,* finely chopped

1 large tomato, seeded and chopped

½ teaspoon salt

⅛ teaspoon black pepper

Hot pepper sauce (optional)

Jalapeño peppers can sting and irritate the skin, so wear rubber gloves when handling peppers and do not touch your eyes.

1. Sort and rinse beans; cover with water. Soak 8 hours or overnight. Drain.

2. Combine beans and broth in large saucepan; bring to a boil over high heat. Add bay leaf. Reduce heat to low; cover and simmer 1½ hours or until beans are tender.

3. Heat oil in large nonstick skillet over medium heat. Add onion, bell peppers, garlic and jalapeño; cook and stir 8 to 10 minutes or until onion is translucent. Add tomato, salt and black pepper; cook 5 minutes.

4. Add onion mixture to beans; cook 15 to 20 minutes.

5. Remove and discard bay leaf. Serve with hot pepper sauce, if desired.

Makes 6 servings

Nutrients per Serving (½ cup): Calories: 146, Total Fat: 2g, Saturated Fat: <1g, Cholesterol: 0mg, Sodium: 209mg, Carbohydrate: 24g, Fiber: 6g, Protein: 8g

confetti black beans

lemon-tossed linguine

8 ounces uncooked linguine noodles

3 tablespoons lemon juice

2 teaspoons reduced-fat margarine

2 tablespoons minced chives

⅓ cup fat-free (skim) milk

1 teaspoon cornstarch

1 tablespoon minced fresh dill sprigs *or* 1 teaspoon dried dill weed

1 tablespoon minced fresh parsley *or* 1 teaspoon dried parsley flakes

2 teaspoons grated lemon peel

¼ teaspoon ground white pepper

3 tablespoons grated Romano or Parmesan cheese

Additional fresh dill sprigs and lemon slices (optional)

1. Cook linguine according to package directions, omitting salt and fat. Drain. Place in medium bowl; sprinkle with lemon juice.

2. Melt margarine in small saucepan over medium heat. Add chives; cook until tender. Whisk milk and cornstarch in small bowl until smooth and well blended; stir into saucepan. Cook and stir until sauce is thickened. Stir in 1 tablespoon dill, parsley, lemon peel and white pepper.

3. Pour milk mixture over noodles. Sprinkle with cheese; toss to coat evenly. Garnish with additional fresh dill sprigs and lemon slices. Serve immediately. *Makes 3 servings*

Nutrients per Serving (½ cup): Calories: 173, Total Fat: 3g, Saturated Fat: 1g, Cholesterol: 7mg, Sodium: 110mg, Carbohydrate: 27g, Fiber: 2g, Protein: 8g

lemon-tossed linguine

spirited sweet potato casserole

2½ pounds sweet potatoes
2 tablespoons margarine
⅓ cup low-fat (1%) or fat-free (skim) milk
¼ cup packed brown sugar
2 tablespoons bourbon or apple juice
1 teaspoon ground cinnamon
1 teaspoon vanilla
2 egg whites
½ teaspoon salt
⅓ cup chopped pecans
3 whole pecans (optional)

1. Preheat oven to 375°F. Bake sweet potatoes 50 to 60 minutes or until very tender. Cool 10 minutes. Leave oven on.

2. Scoop pulp from warm potatoes into large bowl; discard skins. Add margarine; mash with potato masher until smooth and margarine is melted. Stir in milk, brown sugar, bourbon, cinnamon and vanilla.

3. Beat egg whites in medium bowl with electric mixer at high speed until soft peaks form. Add salt; beat until stiff peaks form. Gently fold egg whites into sweet potato mixture.

4. Spray 1½-quart soufflé dish with nonstick cooking spray. Spoon sweet potato mixture into dish; sprinkle chopped pecans around edge of dish. Arrange whole pecans in center, if desired.

5. Bake 30 to 35 minutes or until soufflé is puffed and pecans are toasted. Serve immediately. *Makes 8 servings*

Nutrients per Serving (⅛ of total recipe): Calories: 203, Total Fat: 5g, Saturated Fat: 1g, Cholesterol: <1mg, Sodium: 202mg, Carbohydrate: 35g, Fiber: <1g, Protein: 3g

spirited sweet potato casserole

tomato, avocado and cucumber salad with feta cheese

1½ tablespoons extra virgin olive oil
1 tablespoon balsamic vinegar
1 clove garlic, minced
¼ teaspoon salt
¼ teaspoon black pepper
2 cups diced seeded plum tomatoes
1 small ripe avocado, peeled, seeded and diced to ½-inch chunks
½ cup chopped cucumber
⅓ cup crumbled reduced-fat feta cheese
4 large red leaf lettuce leaves
Chopped fresh basil (optional)

1. Whisk oil, vinegar, garlic, salt and pepper in medium bowl. Add tomatoes and avocado; toss to coat evenly. Gently stir in cucumber and feta cheese.

2. Arrange 1 lettuce leaf on each serving plate. Spoon salad evenly onto lettuce leaves. Top with basil, if desired.   *Makes 4 servings*

Nutrients per Serving (¼ of total recipe): Calories: 138, Total Fat: 11g, Saturated Fat: 2g, Cholesterol: 3mg, Sodium: 311mg, Carbohydrate: 7g, Fiber: 2g, Protein: 4g

fresh corn sauté

2 teaspoons canola or olive oil
½ cup chopped sweet or yellow onion
½ cup chopped red bell pepper
2 cups fresh corn kernels (3 to 4 ears corn) *or* 1 package
    (10 ounces) frozen corn kernels, thawed
¼ teaspoon salt (optional)
2 tablespoons imitation bacon bits

Heat oil in medium saucepan over medium heat. Add onion and bell pepper; cook and stir 4 minutes. Add corn and salt, if desired; cook and stir 2 minutes or until vegetables are crisp-tender. Stir in bacon bits.

Makes 4 servings

Nutrients per Serving (½ cup): Calories: 115, Total Fat: 4g, Saturated Fat: <1g, Cholesterol: 0mg, Sodium: 64mg, Carbohydrate: 20g, Fiber: 3g, Protein: 4g

tomato, avocado and cucumber salad with feta cheese

potato-zucchini pancakes

1 medium baking potato, unpeeled and shredded
½ small zucchini, shredded
1 green onion, thinly sliced, plus additional for garnish
1 egg white
2 tablespoons all-purpose flour
1 tablespoon vegetable oil
  Sour cream (optional)

1. Combine potato, zucchini, 1 green onion, egg white and flour in medium bowl; mix well.

2. Heat oil in large nonstick skillet over medium heat. Drop ⅓ cupfuls potato mixture into skillet; flatten slightly. Cook 5 minutes per side or until browned.

3. Serve with sour cream, if desired. Garnish with additional green onion.

Makes 2 servings

Nutrients per Serving (3 pancakes): Calories: 190, Total Fat: 7g, Saturated Fat: 1g, Cholesterol: 0mg, Sodium: 40mg, Carbohydrate: 27g, Fiber: 2g, Protein: 6g

Tip: Save time by shredding both the potato and zucchini in a food processor fitted with a shredding disc.

potato-zucchini pancakes

chile and lime quinoa

½ **cup quinoa**

1 **cup water**

1 **small jalapeño pepper, minced***

2 **tablespoons finely chopped green onion**

2 **tablespoons olive oil**

1 **tablespoon fresh lime juice**

¼ **teaspoon salt**

¼ **teaspoon ground cumin**

¼ **teaspoon chili powder**

⅛ **teaspoon black pepper**

*Jalapeño peppers can sting and irritate the skin, so wear rubber gloves when handling peppers and do not touch your eyes.

1. Place quinoa in fine-mesh strainer; rinse well under cold running water.

2. Combine quinoa and water in small saucepan; bring to a boil over high heat. Reduce heat to low; cover and simmer 12 to 15 minutes or until quinoa is tender. Drain. Cover; let stand 5 minutes.

3. Stir jalapeño, green onion, oil, lime juice, salt, cumin, chili powder and black pepper into quinoa. Fluff mixture with fork. Serve warm or at room temperature. *Makes 4 servings*

Nutrients per Serving (½ cup): Calories: 144, Total Fat: 8g, Saturated Fat: 1g, Cholesterol: 0mg, Sodium: 153mg, Carbohydrate: 16g, Fiber: 2g, Protein: 3g

Note: Quinoa is a high-protein grain with a flavor similar to couscous. It cooks more quickly than rice and has less carbohydrates than any other grain. Look for it in the rice and dried beans section or in the natural foods aisle of the supermarket.

chile and lime quinoa

old-fashioned herb stuffing

6 slices (8 ounces) whole wheat, rye or white bread (or combination), cut into ½-inch cubes
1 tablespoon margarine or butter
1 cup chopped onion
½ cup thinly sliced celery
½ cup thinly sliced carrot
1 cup fat-free reduced-sodium chicken broth
1 tablespoon chopped fresh thyme *or* 1 teaspoon dried thyme
1 tablespoon chopped fresh sage *or* 1 teaspoon dried sage
½ teaspoon paprika
¼ teaspoon black pepper

1. Preheat oven to 350°F. Place bread cubes on baking sheet; bake 10 minutes or until dry.

2. Spray 1½-quart baking dish with nonstick cooking spray.

3. Melt margarine in large saucepan over medium heat. Add onion, celery and carrot; cook and stir 10 minutes or until vegetables are tender. Add broth, thyme, sage, paprika and pepper to saucepan; bring to a simmer. Stir in bread cubes. Spoon into prepared dish.

4. Cover; bake 25 to 30 minutes or until heated through.

Makes 4 servings

Nutrients per Serving (¼ of total recipe): Calories: 199, Total Fat: 5g, Saturated Fat: 1g, Cholesterol: 0mg, Sodium: 395mg, Carbohydrate: 32g, Fiber: 5g, Protein: 8g

old-fashioned herb stuffing

orzo with spinach and red pepper

4 ounces uncooked orzo pasta

1 teaspoon olive oil

1 medium red bell pepper, diced

3 cloves garlic, minced

1 package (10 ounces) frozen chopped spinach, thawed and squeezed dry

¼ cup grated Parmesan cheese

½ teaspoon finely chopped fresh oregano or basil (optional)

¼ teaspoon lemon pepper

1. Prepare orzo according to package directions, omitting salt and fat. Drain; set aside.

2. Heat oil in large nonstick skillet over medium-high heat. Add bell pepper and garlic; cook and stir 2 to 3 minutes or until bell pepper is crisp-tender. Add orzo and spinach; cook and stir until heated through. Remove from heat.

3. Stir in cheese, oregano, if desired, and lemon pepper. Serve immediately.

Makes 6 servings

Nutrients per Serving (⅙ of total recipe): Calories: 116, Total Fat: 3g, Saturated Fat: 1g, Cholesterol: 3mg, Sodium: 152mg, Carbohydrate: 19g, Fiber: 2g, Protein: 6g

orzo with spinach and red pepper

southern macaroni and cheese

        2 teaspoons all-purpose flour
        1 tablespoon dry mustard
        ½ teaspoon salt
        ½ teaspoon black pepper
        1 cup fat-free (skim) milk
        ½ cup plus 1 tablespoon shredded reduced-fat (2% milk)
            sharp Cheddar cheese, divided
        1 egg white
     1½ cups cooked whole wheat or multigrain elbow macaroni
        1 tablespoon panko or unseasoned bread crumbs*
        ⅛ teaspoon paprika

Panko are Japanese bread crumbs and have less sugar, fat and sodium than regular bread crumbs. They are available in most grocery stores in the Asian section or you can find them in an Asian market.

1. Preheat oven to 325°F. Spray 1-quart baking dish with nonstick cooking spray.

2. Combine flour, mustard, salt and pepper in small saucepan; whisk in milk. Cook and stir over medium heat until mixture is bubbly and thickened. Remove from heat; let stand 2 to 3 minutes. Stir in ½ cup cheese until melted.

3. Stir egg white into macaroni in large bowl. Stir in cheese sauce. Spoon into prepared dish. Combine remaining 1 tablespoon cheese, panko and paprika; mix well. Sprinkle over macaroni.

4. Bake 15 to 20 minutes or until bubbly and lightly browned. Let stand 5 minutes before serving. *Makes 4 servings*

Nutrients per Serving (⅓ cup): Calories: 140, Total Fat: 4g, Saturated Fat: 2g, Cholesterol: 10mg, Sodium: 490mg, Carbohydrate: 19g, Fiber: 2g, Protein: 10g

southern macaroni and cheese

mediterranean-style roasted vegetables

1½ **pounds red potatoes, cut into ½-inch chunks**

1 **tablespoon plus 1½ teaspoons olive oil, divided**

1 **red bell pepper, cut into ½-inch pieces**

1 **yellow or orange bell pepper, cut into ½-inch pieces**

1 **small red onion, cut into ½-inch wedges**

2 **cloves garlic, minced**

½ **teaspoon salt**

¼ **teaspoon black pepper**

1 **tablespoon balsamic vinegar**

¼ **cup chopped fresh basil leaves**

1. Preheat oven to 425°F. Spray large roasting pan with nonstick cooking spray.

2. Place potatoes in prepared pan. Drizzle with 1 tablespoon oil; toss to coat evenly. Roast 10 minutes.

3. Add bell peppers and onion to pan. Drizzle with remaining 1½ teaspoons oil. Sprinkle with garlic, salt and black pepper; toss to coat evenly.

4. Roast 18 to 20 minutes or until vegetables are browned and tender, stirring once.

5. Transfer vegetables to large serving dish. Drizzle vinegar over vegetables; toss to coat evenly. Add basil; toss again. Serve warm or at room temperature. *Makes 6 servings*

Nutrients per Serving (⅙ of total recipe): Calories: 170, Total Fat: 4g, Saturated Fat: <1g, Cholesterol: 0mg, Sodium: 185mg, Carbohydrate: 33g, Fiber: 1g, Protein: 3g

mediterranean-style roasted vegetables

oven "fries"

2 small russet potatoes (10 ounces), refrigerated
2 teaspoons olive oil
¼ teaspoon salt or onion salt

1. Preheat oven to 450°F. Peel potatoes and cut lengthwise into ¼-inch strips. Place in colander; rinse under cold running water 2 minutes. Drain. Pat dry with paper towels.

2. Place potatoes in small resealable food storage bag. Drizzle with oil. Seal bag; shake to coat evenly. Arrange potatoes in single layer on baking sheet

3. Bake 20 to 25 minutes or until light brown and crisp. Sprinkle with salt.

Makes 2 servings

Nutrients per Serving (½ of fries): Calories: 237, Total Fat: 7g, Saturated Fat: 1g, Cholesterol: 0mg, Sodium: 300mg, Carbohydrate: 41g, Fiber: 3g, Protein: 4g

Note: Refrigerating potatoes—usually not recommended for storage—converts the starch in the potatoes to sugar, which enhances the browning when the potatoes are baked. Do not refrigerate the potatoes longer than 2 days, because they may develop a sweet flavor.

oven "fries"

zesty pasta salad

1 cup (about 3 ounces) uncooked tri-color rotini pasta
1 cup sliced fresh mushrooms
¾ cup canned diced tomatoes
½ cup sliced green bell pepper
¼ cup chopped onion
¼ cup fat-free Italian salad dressing
2 tablespoons freshly grated Parmesan cheese

1. Cook pasta according to package directions, omitting salt and fat. Rinse under cool running water. Drain; cool completely.

2. Combine pasta, mushrooms, tomatoes, bell pepper and onion in large bowl. Pour Italian dressing over pasta mixture; toss to coat evenly. Sprinkle with cheese just before serving.   *Makes 6 servings*

Nutrients per Serving (⅙ of total recipe): Calories: 80, Total Fat: 2g, Saturated Fat: <1g, Cholesterol: 2mg, Sodium: 239mg, Carbohydrate: 13g, Fiber: 1g, Protein: 4g

spiced rice and carrot salad

⅔ cup cooked brown rice, chilled
2 medium carrots, shredded
1 green onion, chopped
1 teaspoon white vinegar
1 teaspoon canola oil
1 teaspoon Chinese chili-garlic sauce
⅛ teaspoon salt
⅛ teaspoon black pepper

Combine rice, carrots and green onion in medium bowl. Whisk vinegar, oil, chili-garlic sauce, salt and pepper in small bowl until well blended. Stir into rice mixture. Serve immediately or cover and refrigerate until ready to serve.   *Makes 2 servings*

Nutrients per Serving (¾ cup): Calories: 275, Total Fat: 4g, Saturated Fat: <1g, Cholesterol: 0mg, Sodium: 236mg, Carbohydrate: 55g, Fiber: 5g, Protein: 6g

zesty pasta salad

Desserts

pineapple coconut cupcakes

1 package (about 18 ounces) white cake mix
1 can (12 ounces) sugar-free lemon-lime soda
1 egg
1 egg white
2 tablespoons canola oil
½ cup sweetened flaked coconut, toasted*
1 can (20 ounces) crushed pineapple in its own juice
1 tablespoon plus 1 teaspoon cornstarch
2 cups sugar-free whipped topping

*To toast coconut, spread evenly on ungreased baking sheet. Bake in preheated 350°F oven 5 to 7 minutes or until light golden brown, stirring occasionally.

1. Preheat oven according to package directions. Line 24 standard (2½-inch) muffin cups with paper baking cups.

2. Beat cake mix, soda, egg, egg white and oil in large bowl with electric mixer at low speed 30 seconds. Beat at medium speed 2 minutes or until well blended. Spoon evenly into prepared muffin cups.

3. Bake 14 minutes or until toothpick inserted into centers comes out clean. Cool in pans 10 minutes. Remove to wire racks; cool completely.

4. Combine pineapple with juice and cornstarch in medium saucepan; bring to a boil over medium-high heat. Cook and stir 1 minute or until thickened. Remove from heat; cool to room temperature.

5. Spoon 1 tablespoon whipped topping on each cupcake; top with 1 tablespoon pineapple mixture. Sprinkle with toasted coconut. Serve immediately or cover and refrigerate until ready to serve.

Makes 24 cupcakes

Nutrients per Serving (1 cupcake): Calories: 144, Total Fat: 5g, Saturated Fat: 2g, Cholesterol: 9mg, Sodium: 155mg, Carbohydrate: 24g, Fiber: <1g, Protein: 2g

old-fashioned bread pudding

2 cups fat-free (skim) milk

4 egg whites

3 tablespoons sugar

2 tablespoons margarine, melted

1 tablespoon vanilla

2 teaspoons ground cinnamon

12 slices whole wheat bread, cut into ½-inch cubes

½ cup raisins

½ cup chopped dried apples

1. Preheat oven to 350°F. Spray 2-quart casserole with nonstick cooking spray.

2. Whisk milk, egg whites, sugar, margarine, vanilla and cinnamon in large bowl until sugar is dissolved. Stir in bread cubes, raisins and dried apples. Let stand 5 minutes. Spoon into prepared casserole.

3. Bake 35 minutes or until well browned. Cool completely in casserole on wire rack.   *Makes 12 servings*

Nutrients per Serving (¹/₁₂ of total recipe): Calories: 150, Total Fat: 3g, Saturated Fat: 1g, Cholesterol: 1mg, Sodium: 214mg, Carbohydrate: 26g, Fiber: 1g, Protein: 6g

old-fashioned bread pudding

creamy cappuccino frozen dessert

1 package (8 ounces) cream cheese, softened

1 can (14 ounces) sweetened condensed milk

½ cup chocolate syrup

1 tablespoon instant coffee granules

1 tablespoon hot water

1½ cups thawed frozen whipped topping

1 (6 ounces) chocolate cookie crumb pie crust

¼ cup chopped pecans, toasted*

Additional chocolate syrup

To toast pecans, spread in a single layer on ungreased baking sheet. Bake in preheated 350°F oven 8 to 10 minutes or until fragrant, stirring occasionally.

1. Beat cream cheese in large bowl with electric mixer at medium speed 2 to 3 minutes or until fluffy. Add sweetened condensed milk and ½ cup chocolate syrup; beat at low speed until well blended.

2. Dissolve coffee granules in hot water in small bowl. Slowly stir into cream cheese mixture. Fold in whipped topping; spoon mixture into crust. Sprinkle with pecans. Cover and freeze overnight.

3. Let dessert stand in refrigerator 10 to 15 minutes before serving. Cut into wedges. Drizzle with additional syrup.   *Makes 16 servings*

Nutrients per Serving (1 wedge): Calories: 230, Total Fat: 12g, Saturated Fat: 6g, Cholesterol: 25mg, Sodium: 150mg, Carbohydrate: 29g, Fiber: 1g, Protein: 4g

creamy cappuccino frozen dessert

butterscotch bars

¾ cup all-purpose flour

½ cup packed brown sugar

½ cup chopped pecans, toasted (optional)*

¼ teaspoon salt

½ cup fat-free butterscotch ice cream topping

¼ cup cholesterol-free egg substitute

3 tablespoons margarine or butter, melted

1 teaspoon vanilla

*To toast pecans, spread in a single layer on ungreased baking sheet. Bake in preheated 350°F oven 8 to 10 minutes or until fragrant, stirring occasionally.

1. Preheat oven to 350°F. Spray 8-inch square baking pan with nonstick cooking spray.

2. Combine flour, brown sugar, pecans, if desired, and salt in large bowl; mix well. Whisk ice cream topping, egg substitute, margarine and vanilla in small bowl until well blended. Stir into flour mixture until well blended. Pour into prepared pan.

3. Bake 15 to 18 minutes or until firm. Cool completely in pan on wire rack. Cut into bars.   *Makes 16 bars*

Nutrients per Serving (1 bar): Calories: 103, Total Fat: 2g, Saturated Fat: <1g, Cholesterol: 6mg, Sodium: 90mg, Carbohydrate: 19g, Fiber: <1g, Protein: 1g

Tip: These sweet bars are the perfect packable treat. Wrap individually in plastic wrap so they will be ready to grab for the lunch box.

butterscotch bars

apple galette

¾ cup all-purpose flour

¼ cup whole wheat flour

1 teaspoon baking powder

⅛ teaspoon salt

¼ cup (½ stick) cold margarine

3 tablespoons plus 1 teaspoon cold fat-free (skim) milk, divided

3 cups thinly sliced peeled baking apples

2 tablespoons sugar

1 teaspoon ground cinnamon

1. Preheat oven to 375°F.

2. Combine all-purpose flour, whole wheat flour, baking powder and salt in medium bowl; mix well. Cut in margarine with pastry blender or two knives until mixture resembles coarse crumbs. Add 3 tablespoons milk, 1 tablespoon at a time, mixing with fork until dough is moistened. (Dough will be crumbly.)

3. Turn dough out on lightly floured surface; knead 6 to 8 times or just until dough clings together. Shape into ball; roll into 12-inch circle on heavy-duty foil. Transfer dough with foil to large baking sheet.

4. Combine apples, sugar and cinnamon in medium bowl; toss to coat evenly. Mound apple mixture in center of dough, leaving 2-inch border. Fold border up over filling. Brush top and side of crust with remaining 1 teaspoon milk. Cover edge of crust with foil.

5. Bake 15 minutes; remove foil. Bake 25 minutes or until crust is golden and apples are tender. Cool on baking sheet 10 minutes. Remove to wire rack; cool 20 minutes. Serve warm. *Makes 6 servings*

Nutrients per Serving (⅙ of galette): Calories: 190, Total Fat: 8g, Saturated Fat: 2g, Cholesterol: 0mg, Sodium: 210mg, Carbohydrate: 28g, Fiber: 2g, Protein: 3g

apple galette

special treat no-bake squares

½ cup (1 stick) plus 1 teaspoon butter, divided
¼ cup granulated sugar
¼ cup unsweetened cocoa powder
1 egg
¼ teaspoon salt
1½ cups graham cracker crumbs
¾ cup flaked coconut
½ cup chopped pecans
⅓ cup butter, softened
1 package (3 ounces) cream cheese, softened
1 teaspoon vanilla
1 cup powdered sugar
1 (2-ounce) dark sweet or bittersweet chocolate candy bar, broken
   into ½-inch pieces

1. Line 9-inch square baking pan with foil, allowing 2-inch overhang on all sides.

2. Cook and stir ½ cup butter, sugar, cocoa, egg and salt in medium saucepan over medium heat 2 minutes or until mixture is thickened. Remove from heat; stir in graham cracker crumbs, coconut and pecans. Press mixture into prepared pan.

3. Beat ⅓ cup softened butter, cream cheese and vanilla in small bowl until smooth and well blended. Gradually add powdered sugar, beating well after each addition. Spread over prepared crust; refrigerate 30 minutes.

4. Combine candy bar and remaining 1 teaspoon butter in small resealable food storage bag; seal bag. Microwave on HIGH 1 minute. Turn bag; microwave on HIGH 30 to 40 seconds or until melted and smooth. Cut off tiny corner of bag; drizzle chocolate mixture over filling.

5. Refrigerate 20 minutes or until firm. Remove from pan using foil. Cut into squares. *Makes about 3 dozen squares*

Nutrients per Serving (1 square): Calories: 110, Total Fat: 8g, Saturated Fat: 4g, Cholesterol: 20mg, Sodium: 50mg, Carbohydrate: 10g, Fiber: 1g, Protein: 1g

special treat no-bake squares

deep, dark gingerbread rounds

1 package (about 14 ounces) gingerbread cake and cookie mix
2 cans (8 ounces each) crushed pineapple in juice, drained
2 jars (4 ounces each) baby food puréed sweet potatoes
2 egg whites *or* **¼ cup egg substitute**
½ cup reduced-fat cream cheese

1. Preheat oven to 325°F. Spray 24 standard (2½-inch) muffin cups with nonstick cooking spray.

2. Combine gingerbread mix, pineapple, sweet potatoes and egg whites in medium bowl; stir just until blended. Spoon evenly into prepared muffin cups.

3. Bake 25 minutes or until toothpick inserted into centers comes out clean. Remove to wire racks; cool completely.

4. To serve, top each cake round with 1 teaspoon cream cheese.

Makes 24 servings

Nutrients per Serving (1 round with about 1 teaspoon cream cheese):
Calories: 105, Total Fat: 3g, Saturated Fat: 1g, Cholesterol: 3mg, Sodium: 144mg, Carbohydrate: 17g, Fiber: 1g, Protein: 2g

Note: These cake rounds taste even better the next day!   3pts

deep, dark gingerbread round

chocolate-frosted peanut butter cupcakes

1¾ cups all-purpose flour

1½ teaspoons baking powder

¼ teaspoon salt

⅓ cup (⅔ stick) butter, softened

⅓ cup creamy or chunky reduced-fat peanut butter

½ cup granulated sugar

¼ cup packed brown sugar

2 eggs

1 teaspoon vanilla

1¼ cups milk

Chocolate Peanut Butter Frosting (page 174)

1. Preheat oven to 350°F. Line 18 standard (2½-inch) muffin cups with paper or foil baking cups.

2. Combine flour, baking powder and salt in medium bowl; mix well. Beat butter and peanut butter in large bowl with electric mixer at medium speed until smooth. Add granulated sugar and brown sugar; beat until well blended. Add eggs and vanilla; beat until well blended. Alternately add flour mixture and milk, beating well after each addition. Spoon evenly into prepared muffin cups.

3. Bake 25 minutes or until toothpick inserted into centers comes out clean. Cool in pans 10 minutes. Remove to wire racks; cool completely.

4. Prepare Chocolate Peanut Butter Frosting. Frost cupcakes.

Makes 18 cupcakes

Nutrients per Serving (1 cupcake): Calories: 201, Total Fat: 7g, Saturated Fat: 2g, Cholesterol: 18mg, Sodium: 134mg, Carbohydrate: 32g, Fiber: 1g, Protein: 4g

Tip: If you don't have muffin pans, don't worry. Foil baking cups are sturdy enough to be used without muffin pans; simply place the baking cups on a baking sheet and fill with batter.

continued on page 174

chocolate-frosted peanut butter cupcake

chocolate-frosted peanut butter cupcakes, continued

chocolate peanut butter frosting

4 cups powdered sugar
⅓ cup unsweetened cocoa powder
4 to 6 tablespoons milk, divided
3 tablespoons creamy peanut butter

Beat powdered sugar, cocoa, 4 tablespoons milk and peanut butter in large bowl with electric mixer at low speed until smooth. Beat in additional milk, 1 tablespoon at a time, until desired spreading consistency is reached. *Makes about 2½ cups*

apricot crumb bars

1 package (about 18 ounces) light yellow cake mix
1 teaspoon ground cinnamon
½ teaspoon ground nutmeg
¼ cup plus 2 tablespoons cold margarine, cut into pieces
¾ cup uncooked multigrain oatmeal cereal or old-fashioned oats
1 egg
2 egg whites
1 tablespoon water
1 jar (10 ounces) apricot fruit spread
2 tablespoons packed light brown sugar

1. Preheat oven to 350°F.

2. Combine cake mix, cinnamon and nutmeg in medium bowl. Cut in margarine with pastry blender or two knives until mixture resembles coarse crumbs. Stir in cereal. Reserve 1 cup crumb mixture. Add egg, egg whites and water to remaining crumb mixture; stir until well blended.

3. Spread mixture evenly into ungreased 13×9-inch baking pan; top evenly with fruit spread. Sprinkle with reserved crumb mixture and brown sugar.

4. Bake 35 to 40 minutes or until top is golden brown. Cool completely in pan on wire rack. Cut into bars. *Makes 15 bars*

Nutrients per Serving (1 bar): Calories: 267, Total Fat: 7g, Saturated Fat: 2g, Cholesterol: 14mg, Sodium: 299mg, Carbohydrate: 48g, Fiber: 1g, Protein: 2g

blueberry custard supreme

½ **cup fresh blueberries**

2 **tablespoons all-purpose flour**

1½ **tablespoons granulated sugar**

¼ **teaspoon ground cardamom**

⅛ **teaspoon salt**

¾ **cup reduced-fat (2%) milk**

¼ **cup cholesterol-free egg substitute**

1 **teaspoon grated lemon peel**

½ **teaspoon vanilla**

1 **teaspoon powdered sugar**

1. Preheat oven to 350°F. Spray 1-quart casserole or soufflé dish with nonstick cooking spray. Spread blueberries in prepared casserole.

2. Combine flour, granulated sugar, cardamom and salt in small bowl; mix well. Stir in milk, egg substitute, lemon peel and vanilla until smooth and well blended. Pour over blueberries.

3. Bake 30 minutes or until puffed, lightly browned and center is set. Cool in casserole on wire rack 10 minutes.

4. Serve warm or at room temperature. Sprinkle with powdered sugar just before serving. *Makes 2 servings*

Nutrients per Serving (1 custard): Calories: 155, Total Fat: 2g, Saturated Fat: 1g, Cholesterol: 7mg, Sodium: 249mg, Carbohydrate: 27g, Fiber: 1g, Protein: 7g

Blackberry Custard Supreme: Substitute fresh blackberries for the blueberries.

banana pudding squares

1 cup graham cracker crumbs

2 tablespoons margarine, melted

1 package (8 ounces) fat-free cream cheese, softened

3 cups fat-free (skim) milk

2 packages (4-serving size) banana cream fat-free sugar-free instant pudding and pie filling mix

1 container (8 ounces) reduced-fat whipped topping, divided

2 medium bananas

1. Line 13×9-inch pan with foil; spray with nonstick cooking spray.

2. Stir graham cracker crumbs and margarine in small bowl until well blended. Press mixture into prepared pan.

3. Beat cream cheese in large bowl with electric mixer at low speed until smooth. Add milk and pudding mix; beat at high speed 2 minutes or until smooth and creamy. Fold half of whipped topping into pudding until well blended. Reserve half of pudding mixture. Spread remaining pudding mixture over crust.

4. Peel bananas; cut into ¼-inch slices. Arrange bananas evenly over pudding layer. Spoon reserved pudding mixture over bananas. Spread remaining whipped topping evenly over pudding mixture.

5. Loosely cover with plastic wrap and refrigerate 2 hours or up to 8 hours.

Makes 18 servings

Nutrients per Serving (1 square): Calories: 112, Total Fat: 4g, Saturated Fat: 2g, Cholesterol: 2mg, Sodium: 292mg, Carbohydrate: 15g, Fiber: 1g, Protein: 4g

banana pudding square

chewy mocha brownie cookies

- 1 cup all-purpose flour
- ¼ teaspoon baking soda
- ¼ cup (½ stick) margarine
- ⅔ cup granulated sugar
- ⅓ cup unsweetened cocoa powder
- ¼ cup packed brown sugar
- 1½ teaspoons instant coffee granules
- ¼ cup low-fat buttermilk
- 1 teaspoon vanilla
- 2 tablespoons powdered sugar

1. Combine flour and baking soda in small bowl; mix well. Melt margarine in medium saucepan; remove from heat. Stir in granulated sugar, cocoa, brown sugar and coffee granules until well blended. Stir in buttermilk and vanilla. Stir in flour mixture just until combined. Transfer to medium bowl. Cover and refrigerate 1 hour. (Dough will be stiff.)

2. Preheat oven to 350°F. Spray cookie sheets with nonstick cooking spray or line with parchment paper. Drop dough by rounded teaspoonfuls onto prepared cookie sheets.

3. Bake 10 to 11 minutes or until edges are firm. Cool on cookie sheets 2 minutes. Remove to wire racks; cool completely.

4. Sprinkle with powdered sugar just before serving.

Makes about 2 dozen cookies

Nutrients per Serving (2 cookies): Calories: 142, Total Fat: 4g, Saturated Fat: 1g, Cholesterol: 0mg, Sodium: 69mg, Carbohydrate: 26g, Fiber: 1g, Protein: 2g

chewy mocha brownie cookies

lemon-ginger apple crisp

6 cups peeled apple slices

¼ cup plus 2 tablespoons packed brown sugar, divided

3 tablespoons all-purpose flour, divided

2 tablespoons lemon juice

1 teaspoon grated lemon peel

½ teaspoon ground ginger

¼ cup quick oats

1 tablespoon margarine, melted

1. Preheat oven to 350°F.

2. Combine apples, ¼ cup brown sugar, 1 tablespoon flour, lemon juice, lemon peel and ginger in 2-quart ovenproof microwavable baking dish; toss to coat evenly.

3. Combine remaining 2 tablespoons brown sugar, 2 tablespoons flour, oats and margarine in small bowl; mix well. Sprinkle evenly over apple mixture.

4. Microwave on HIGH 12 to 15 minutes or until mixture begins to bubble.

5. Bake 15 to 20 minutes or until apples are tender and topping is golden brown. *Makes 6 servings*

Nutrients per Serving (⅙ of total recipe): Calories: 179, Total Fat: 3g, Saturated Fat: 0g, Cholesterol: 0mg, Sodium: 26mg, Carbohydrate: 38g, Fiber: 3g, Protein: 1g

lemon-ginger apple crisp

quick chocolate chip cookie cakes

1 package (about 18 ounces) reduced-fat yellow cake mix
½ cup cholesterol-free egg substitute
¼ cup vegetable oil
¼ cup reduced-fat sour cream
2 cups old-fashioned oats
½ cup semisweet chocolate chips

1. Preheat oven to 350°F. Spray cookie sheets with nonstick cooking spray.

2. Combine cake mix, egg substitute, oil and sour cream in medium bowl; mix well. Stir in oats and chocolate chips. Drop dough by teaspoonfuls onto prepared cookie sheets.

3. Bake 12 minutes or until lightly browned. Remove to wire racks; cool completely. *Makes about 4 dozen cookie cakes*

Nutrients per Serving (1 cookie cake): Calories: 79, Total Fat: 3g, Saturated Fat: 1g, Cholesterol: <1mg, Sodium: 74mg, Carbohydrate: 13g, Fiber: <1g, Protein: 1g

quick chocolate chip cookie cakes

chocolate buttons

10 dates, pitted and chopped
½ cup water
¼ cup (½ stick) soft baking butter with canola oil
¼ cup chopped bittersweet chocolate
1½ cups all-purpose flour
½ teaspoon baking soda
⅛ teaspoon salt
¼ cup packed dark brown sugar
¼ cup fat-free sour cream
1 tablespoon unsweetened cocoa powder

1. Preheat oven to 350°F.

2. Combine dates and water in small saucepan. Cover; bring to a boil over high heat. Reduce heat to medium; simmer 1 minute or until dates are soft. Place dates and cooking liquid in food processor or blender; process until smooth. (Mixture will be pasty.)

3. Melt butter and chocolate in small saucepan over low heat, stirring constantly. Remove from heat.

4. Combine flour, baking soda and salt in medium bowl; mix well. Beat date mixture, chocolate mixture, brown sugar and sour cream in large bowl with electric mixer at medium speed 2 minutes or until well blended. Add flour mixture; beat at low speed until well blended.

5. Drop dough by teaspoonfuls onto ungreased cookie sheets. Sprinkle with cocoa.

6. Bake 6 minutes or just until set. *Do not overbake.* Cool on cookie sheets 2 minutes. Remove to wire racks; cool completely.

Makes about 6 dozen cookies

Nutrients per Serving (1 cookie): Calories: 25, Total Fat: 1g, Saturated Fat: <1g, Cholesterol: 2mg, Sodium: 19mg, Carbohydrate: 5g, Fiber: <1g, Protein: <1g

chocolate buttons

berry bundt cake

2 cups all-purpose flour
1 tablespoon baking powder
1 teaspoon baking soda
¼ teaspoon salt
1 cup sugar
¾ cup buttermilk
½ cup cholesterol-free egg substitute
¼ cup vegetable oil
2 cups frozen unsweetened raspberries
2 cups frozen unsweetened blueberries

1. Preheat oven to 350°F. Spray 6-cup bundt pan with nonstick cooking spray.

2. Combine flour, baking powder, baking soda and salt in large bowl; mix well. Whisk sugar, buttermilk, egg substitute and oil in medium bowl until well blended. Add sugar mixture to flour mixture; stir just until moistened. Fold in raspberries and blueberries. Pour into prepared pan.

3. Bake 1 hour or until toothpick inserted near center comes out clean. Cool completely in pan on wire rack. *Makes 12 servings*

Nutrients per Serving (1 slice): Calories: 215, Total Fat: 5g, Saturated Fat: 1g, Cholesterol: 1mg, Sodium: 262mg, Carbohydrate: 39g, Fiber: 2g, Protein: 4g

berry bundt cake

METRIC CONVERSION CHART

VOLUME MEASUREMENTS (dry)

1/8 teaspoon = 0.5 mL
1/4 teaspoon = 1 mL
1/2 teaspoon = 2 mL
3/4 teaspoon = 4 mL
1 teaspoon = 5 mL
1 tablespoon = 15 mL
2 tablespoons = 30 mL
1/4 cup = 60 mL
1/3 cup = 75 mL
1/2 cup = 125 mL
2/3 cup = 150 mL
3/4 cup = 175 mL
1 cup = 250 mL
2 cups = 1 pint = 500 mL
3 cups = 750 mL
4 cups = 1 quart = 1 L

VOLUME MEASUREMENTS (fluid)

1 fluid ounce (2 tablespoons) = 30 mL
4 fluid ounces (1/2 cup) = 125 mL
8 fluid ounces (1 cup) = 250 mL
12 fluid ounces (1 1/2 cups) = 375 mL
16 fluid ounces (2 cups) = 500 mL

WEIGHTS (mass)

1/2 ounce = 15 g
1 ounce = 30 g
3 ounces = 90 g
4 ounces = 120 g
8 ounces = 225 g
10 ounces = 285 g
12 ounces = 360 g
16 ounces = 1 pound = 450 g

DIMENSIONS

1/16 inch = 2 mm
1/8 inch = 3 mm
1/4 inch = 6 mm
1/2 inch = 1.5 cm
3/4 inch = 2 cm
1 inch = 2.5 cm

OVEN TEMPERATURES

250°F = 120°C
275°F = 140°C
300°F = 150°C
325°F = 160°C
350°F = 180°C
375°F = 190°C
400°F = 200°C
425°F = 220°C
450°F = 230°C

BAKING PAN SIZES

Utensil	Size in Inches/Quarts	Metric Volume	Size in Centimeters
Baking or Cake Pan (square or rectangular)	8×8×2	2 L	20×20×5
	9×9×2	2.5 L	23×23×5
	12×8×2	3 L	30×20×5
	13×9×2	3.5 L	33×23×5
Loaf Pan	8×4×3	1.5 L	20×10×7
	9×5×3	2 L	23×13×7
Round Layer Cake Pan	8×1½	1.2 L	20×4
	9×1½	1.5 L	23×4
Pie Plate	8×1¼	750 mL	20×3
	9×1¼	1 L	23×3
Baking Dish or Casserole	1 quart	1 L	—
	1½ quart	1.5 L	—
	2 quart	2 L	—